ord alive

In-depth Small Group
Bible Studies

STUDY
GUIDE

James

MW00681620

JAMES

living on
the edge

William C. De Vries

FAITH
ALIVE®
Christian Resources

Grand Rapids, Michigan

Cover photo: Taxi

Word Alive: In-depth Small Group Bible Studies
James: Living on the Edge (Study Guide), © 1994, 2004 (Revised Edition) by Faith
Alive Christian Resources, 2850 Kalamazoo Ave. SE, Grand Rapids, MI 49560.
All rights reserved. With the exception of brief excerpts for review purposes, no
part of this book may be reproduced in any manner whatsoever without written
permission from the publisher. Printed in the United States of America on
recycled paper.

Note: This study material is revised from the Revelation Series format in which it
was published in 1994. "Additional Notes" sections in this study guide were
written by Verlyn Verbrugge, author of the leader's guide for this study.

We welcome your comments. Call us at 1-800-333-8300 or e-mail us at
editors@faithaliveresources.org.

www.FaithAliveResources.org

ISBN 1-56212-984-8

10 9 8 7 6 5 4 3 2

Contents

Contents

Introduction

Greet your trials with joy. Persevere when your faith is tested. Be mature and complete. Ask God for wisdom. Never say, "God is tempting me." Be quick to listen, slow to speak, and slow to become angry. Don't just listen to God's Word; do what it says. Live by the law that gives freedom. Care for the needy.

James, a master of illustration and proverb, says all this in just the first chapter of his letter to Christians who needed encouragement and direction. James's first readers were first-century Christians who were being persecuted for their faith. In some ways they were also persecuting each other.

These Christians were made up of rich and poor, foolish and wise, proud and humble. And although they lived almost two thousand years ago, we easily identify with them because we share many of their struggles and weaknesses.

James speaks to these believers as their pastor. He's familiar with their weaknesses—their bad theology, favoritism, gossip, greed, and grumbling. He also knows they need to be rid of these troubles if they're going to survive faith-testing trials. So James addresses their weak points and shows them how to grow to maturity in faith. He renews their trust in God through Jesus and leads them into vibrant faith and humble action.

Like a pastor, James reminds us too that the goal God is working toward, in Christ, is our maturity as Christians (James 1:4). James shares with us the wisdom of Old Testament Scriptures and many teachings of the "Wisest of the Wise," his brother, Lord, and Savior, Jesus Christ. James teaches us that to hold on to the truth of our hope in Christ, no matter what the consequences, is the heart of true happiness (blessedness). For only in Christ, as the Holy Spirit renews us in the image of our Creator, can our hearts begin to experience and share the deep peace that is pure joy.

—Paul Faber, for Faith Alive Christian Resources

William C. De Vries, author of this study guide, is a minister in the Christian Reformed Church who has served congregations in Ann Arbor, Michigan; Syracuse, New York; and El Paso, Texas. He is currently the pastor of First Christian Reformed Church, Detroit, Michigan.

An accompanying leader's guide written by Verlyn Verbrugge, a Christian Reformed minister who serves as a senior theological editor for Zondervan Corporation, Grand Rapids, Michigan, includes helpful background material and suggestions for leading the discussion of each lesson.

*How do we
react in times
of testing?*

1

JAMES 1:1-12

Joy and Blessing in Tough Times

In a Nutshell

As we begin studying the book of James, we encounter lots of important, practical advice for Christian living—in just the first few opening paragraphs. In line with the Lord Jesus, James is concerned with helping believers become mature in faith, meaning they do not give up on God when tough times threaten. In times of trial and challenge Christians can persevere because the God who gives faith also gives resources for standing firm—and even provides joy and blessing.

James 1:1-12

¹James, a servant of God and of the Lord Jesus Christ,

To the twelve tribes scattered among the nations:

Greetings.

²Consider it pure joy, my brothers, whenever you face trials of many kinds, ³because you know that the testing of your faith develops perseverance. ⁴Perseverance must finish its work so that you may be mature and complete, not lacking anything.

⁵If any of you lacks wisdom, he should ask God, who gives generously to all without finding fault, and it will be given to him.

⁶But when he asks, he must believe and not doubt, because he who doubts is like a wave of the sea, blown and tossed by the wind. ⁷That man should not think he will receive anything from the Lord; ⁸he is a double-minded man, unstable in all he does.

⁹The brother in humble circumstances ought to take pride in his high position. ¹⁰But the one who is rich should take pride in his low position, because he will pass away like a wild flower. ¹¹For the sun rises with scorching heat and withers the plant; its blossom falls and its beauty is destroyed. In the same way, the rich man will fade away even while he goes about his business.

¹²Blessed is the man who perseveres under trial, because when he has stood the

test, he will receive the crown of   those who love him.
life that God has promised to

Strength-Sapping Wonder

Sometimes events just take your breath away. They stop you in your tracks and weaken your knees. Driving north from Alamogordo, New Mexico, can do that. Sierra Blanca Peak rises to more than 12,000 feet on your right as the eerily rolling surface of White Sands Basin drops sharply to your left. The contrasting beauty of the towering green mountain and the glaring white sand is shocking in its power to touch the human spirit.

But not all events of strength-sapping wonder are events of beauty. The sickness of a loved one, the loss of a job, even the daily tensions of interaction with other people can be ugly. Sometimes we lie awake at night with a thousand questions swirling through our minds. In the dark it can often seem that life is dominated by the struggles we face. Fear and anxiety can grip us in menacing silence long after the frustrations and challenges of the day.

Hope and Joy Through Faith

The apostle James teaches us to "consider it pure joy" when we face trials, but that's not all. James also shows us how to do that. "Faith" in "the Lord Jesus Christ" (James 1:1, 3) offers a way of living that enables people to be so renewed that evil cannot make a claim on their lives. James clues us in on how "religion" (1:27) can truly come alive. James shows us religion—*not* religiosity—so deeply attached to the gospel of Christ that faith becomes a way of life, strengthening us to react in hope and even joy when we suffer knee-weakening blows.

One Meaningful I.D.

James must have been a well-known leader in the early church, because nothing more than the mention of his name in this letter is necessary to establish his identity and authority. Quite possibly this was James, the brother of Jesus (Gal. 1:19).

It's interesting to note that James sees only one meaningful identification for himself: he is "a servant" (James 1:1). He thus offers himself as an example of a person who has changed to accept the attitudes and the way of life of a servant of both God and Jesus Christ. When we remember our Lord's warning that no servant can truly serve two masters (Luke 16:13), two important facts come to mind:

- If we are servants of Jesus, we must be obedient to God's ways. A follower of Jesus must follow the way Jesus went, and Jesus held to the purpose and path of God.

- No one can follow God's ways without following Jesus. To truly serve God, one must accept Jesus as Lord in the practical matters of everyday life.

Greeting Trials with Joy

I remember how annoying it was when my children were younger and they'd start to whine about something. That nasal, self-pitying, relentless tone was worse than the screech of fingernails on a blackboard. I tried to let them know that whining hardly approached an effective way to get what they wanted. I'd say that they didn't have to like what was bothering them but that whining only made it worse—for all of us. James urges his readers to go a step further than whining or complaining. He tells us to have joy when tough times come (1:2).

The word for "consider" in James 1:2 can also mean "greet." In a sense, James is teaching that when hard times come to "visit," believers should "greet" them with an underlying joy. And the situation James's first readers faced was far more serious than a matter that might induce whining. These Jewish Christians were under constant pressure and persecution from fellow Jews and from the many Gentile unbelievers around them throughout the Roman Empire. These Christians were hated. Torture and death were not rare events for them. Their lives and livelihoods were often in serious danger.

Because of the seriousness of the trials they faced, and because the Scriptures consistently deal realistically with life, I do not believe James is saying Christians should always smile and act as if nothing is wrong. To behave that way is to deny the reality of suffering and trial. People who love Christ are not called to ignore trials. For example, the death of a loved one causes real hurt, and we should not ask ourselves or others to pretend it doesn't hurt. We can't try to avoid pain by acting as if a hard blow never really happened.

James calls for a broader, deeper perspective and for action that shows a deep awareness of the true direction of trial. Every believer must see that trials, or testing, make a "simple" faith into a "tenacious" faith. That's what James means by "perseverance" (1:3). He's not talking about developing a "stiff upper lip." He sees that for a Christian the critical quality of life is faith. That's why James describes trials as a "testing of [our] faith." We need to see that the events of our lives tone up and deepen our trust in God and in Christ.

James makes clear that the goal God is working toward, in Christ, is our maturity (1:4). Without Christ, we are incomplete. We cannot meet the standards God requires of us as imagebearers of the Creator. But now, in Christ, we are being made to bear God's image completely. This means that in God's power believers can develop all the qualities that make people imagebearers of God.

To gain this completeness, we have to have a faith that is resolute in its trust in God's promises. No effort of our own will bring us to the completion (perfection) that God desires for us. Only a tenacious living faith powered by God will move us to lack nothing of the image of God. And only trials can help us develop the tenacity our faith needs.

As we grasp this wondrous reality, a deep peace, a "pure joy" (1:2), takes hold in the heart of our being. Equipped with this joy about God's will for our perfection, we can greet all kinds of trials in our lives.

Wisdom

But God does not leave us without resources to help us through tough times. James goes on to tell of wisdom that's available to help us grow in maturity and joy. The wisdom we need for dealing productively with trials is true wisdom, which grows from an understanding of our destiny and how it can be affected by the love of God.

God's love for us points in the direction of perfection. It's not that God wants to make people into little gods. Perfection for us does not mean eliminating our humanness. But God does not want to simply leave us as we are. God sent Jesus so that human beings could become all God intends them to be. All the sin that held humanity down is taken away by Jesus' sacrifice. And now a new power is available through the Holy Spirit to shape people into the very character of God.

It takes a special wisdom to see our destiny within God's plan. It takes wisdom that is more than religious thought. It takes wisdom that envelops and shapes the practical decisions of our lives. James says we may expect to receive this wisdom through prayer, by asking God for it (1:5). James also notes that God does not play favorites. God "gives generously to all without finding fault" (1:5). Our great and loving God will certainly not withhold wisdom that would show a believer how God has called him or her to live for the Lord.

Faith

A second resource available to us in maturing as joy-filled Christians is resolute faith. When we ask for wisdom, says James, we "must believe and not doubt" (1:6). James is not reprimanding believers here for having momentary doubts of faith or for having questioning minds. Like the rest of us, James must have known that not every prayer is answered exactly as we might wish. But the reason for this mystery is certainly not that we do not have enough faith, as some people say. That opinion makes God a "player of favorites," and it makes faith out to be a good work by which we earn God's grace and blessing.

Rather than promoting a "works righteousness," James is warning against trying to stand in both the believing and unbelieving camps at the same time. We should not be people who are ready to set aside the Christian life at times. Such people are truly like waves of the sea—now headed this way, now that (1:6). God's gift of wisdom can have little practical effect in our lives if we continually set aside our Christian trust and move in some other direction.

A New Perspective

A third resource for our maturing is a new perspective on our position as Christians. The person who is considered poor in money and goods is often relegated to a low position in society. But if that person is in Christ, he or she is in fact a brother or sister to the King of kings. This true perspective on the importance that comes with being a believer can be a source of righteous pride (1:9). This new perspective frees the believer to pursue a mature, tenacious faith based on all that Jesus has made him or her to be.

James says believers who are rich in money and goods, however, should focus on their low position (1:10). What does that mean? Well, the rich in society never have a low position for long. They are the "movers and shakers" in our world. But James points out that the things society honors will fade and decay. The rich who are in Christ must begin to see themselves first of all as servants. Our Lord taught that all who follow him will be as footwashers on the way to a cross (John 13:14-17; Matt. 16:24). This teaching is a lasting resource of personal value for anyone. We begin to find our source of righteous pride in becoming servants like Jesus. There is no "higher calling" than to serve as Jesus served. Such service establishes our worth and our destiny. It takes us on the same path as the Son of God.

As Christians gain this perspective, they open themselves to God's wisdom. As women and men see that God desires and works to produce a mature, Christlike character in them, their joy in Christ deepens. This joy can carry believers through hard times, though not without tears or pain or passing doubts. It can carry us because it's based on the sure, solid footing of God's great love and desire to make us whole.

Now and Forever

And what will come to the Christian who perseveres through trials greeted with joy in Christ? The Christian who "has stood the test" will enjoy what God desires for us all: a state of blessedness. In a sense, this blessedness may be described as joy and fulfillment that we experience even now in the Christian life (1:2-4).

Let's look for a moment at the phrases "perseveres under trial" and "has stood the test" (1:12). While these phrases together catch the meaning of the original Greek text, a more literal translation points again to the Christian's maturing process. The text includes a sense of "becoming approved." We must understand what is actually happening in the time of trial. Believers in trial are *becoming* what God wants them to be. God's blessing is not guaranteed to people who make it through hard times without cracking emotionally, without suffering financial ruin, or without having their family splinter around them. Blessedness comes to those who become more of what God wants them to be in Christ.

In a sense, then, "the crown of life" is a natural result of the Christian's trials (1:12). The Greek word for "crown" here is the term often used for referring to a laurel wreath of honor and accomplishment worn by a champion athlete or military leader. A crown of honor awaits believers on the other side of whatever hard events are shaping them to be what God wants them to be. What's more, this crown of honor is "the crown of life." It's the assurance of full life, life with meaning. True human honor, which comes to those who have persevered under trial, gives a sense of the fullness of life that believers can have in Christ. This is honor that intertwines with tenacious faith (1:3) and mature completeness before God (1:4).

In another sense, the "crown of life" refers to eternal life, the never-ending life that follows death and is the result also of our Lord's resurrection and promised return. We do not earn the "crown of life" in either this age or the age to come; it is a result of God's promise (1:12).

Additional Notes

1:1—Almost all New Testament commentators agree that James was most likely the brother of Jesus (Gal. 1:19). What do we know about this James? He was probably the oldest of the children that Joseph and Mary had together, since his name is mentioned first in a list of Jesus' brothers (Matt. 13:55). We know that in the early days of Jesus' ministry James did not believe in Jesus (John 7:5). And along with his mother and brothers, James once sought to persuade Jesus to give up his ministry (Matt. 12:46-50; Mark 3:21, 31-35). We do not know when James's transition to faith took place, but he may well be the same James who received a personal visit from Jesus after the resurrection (1 Cor. 15:7). And by the time Jesus' 120 followers were in the upper room waiting for the outpouring of the Holy Spirit, James was there with his other brothers and their mother, Mary (Acts 1:14). James eventually became a leader who was respected as a "pillar" of the church in Jerusalem (see Acts 12:17; 15:13; Gal. 2:9).

1:2-3—It seems clear from these verses that a *peirasmos* ("trial") can be defined as anything that "tests" a person's faith. This Greek word is the same one used to refer to the process of testing metals to see if they are genuine. In this sense we can think of "trials" as the testing ground for determining how genuine our faith is.

The Greek word for "perseverance" comes from a word that literally means "to remain under." So in the context of James's message, a person undergoing a trial will persevere if he or she *remains* faithful to the Lord *under* that trial. (See also 1:12.) Abraham is a prime example of someone who was tested by the Lord and who persevered (see Gen. 22:1-18).

1:5—The "if . . . then" nature of this sentence reflects a condition, but the type of conditional clause used here in the Greek implies that most of us do lack wisdom. So we might better translate the sentence this way: "To the extent that you lack wisdom, you should ask God. . . ."

1:10—The Greek word for "low position" comes from the same word group as "humble" (1:9), so we could read "low position" as "humble status." Note also that James does not say the person's riches will pass away but that *"he* will pass away."

1:12—This is a *beatitude,* a statement that refers to blessedness. Note the similarity of this statement to the beatitude Jesus gives in Matthew 5:11-12. (Ask your leader for a list of several other teachings in James that parallel the sayings of Jesus.)

GENERAL DISCUSSION

1. We all have much to be thankful for. Many of us have to admit, though, that we often spend valuable time and energy whining and complaining. Why do we do that?

2. James mentions facing trials of "many kinds" (1:2). A trial can be anything that puts a strain on your faith. What trials have you had in your life, or what trials can you think of in the lives of others? With the rest of your group, list as many kinds of trials as you can think of. Then, if you wish, share one incident in which you or someone you know has experienced a trial of faith.

3. In what ways can doubt remove us from God's blessings? How is it that in another sense doubt can never remove a Christian from God's blessings?

4. What is "righteous pride"? How does the "righteous pride" of the poor compare with that of the rich?

5. Explain how the promise of the "crown of life" gives real meaning to our lives today. If you like, share one event that has helped you become more of what God wants you to be.

SMALL GROUP SESSION IDEAS

Opening (5-10 minutes)
Pray/Worship—Open your first session of this study with a prayer for God's guidance as you study the book of James. Thank God

for bringing you together for this study, and ask that it may help each of you to grow more and more mature in Christ.

You may wish to engage in a time of worship together by reflecting quietly on ways in which you need to grow in Christ. Spend a minute or two in silent reflection and prayer. Then sing a prayerful hymn that focuses on themes covered in this lesson: faith, perseverance, joy, hope, wisdom, trials, and so on. For example, you could sing together "May the Mind of Christ, My Savior," "Take My Life and Let It Be," "Lord, I Pray," or "O Jesus, Joy of Loving Hearts."

Share—If you're used to meeting together, you'll want to take some time to catch up on how things have been going since you last met. If some or all of you haven't been part of this group before, introduce yourselves and perhaps each share something about yourself that you'd like others in the group to know. For starters, you may want to share with each other the expectations you have as you begin this study of *James: Living on the Edge.*

Focus—The focus question in each lesson is designed to help you begin thinking about the lesson material and how it affects you. Ask yourself one or more of the following questions to help you focus during this session:

- *In what ways has God shaped my faith through tough situations or hard times?*

- *In what other ways has my faith grown?*

- *In what ways do I still need to grow in maturity of faith?*

Growing (35-50 minutes)
Read (optional)—You may want to read James 1:1-12 together (as well as portions of the study guide notes) before moving into a discussion time.

Discuss—While working through the General Discussion questions for this lesson, you may wish to include some of the following process questions, as they fit in with your discussion.

- What sorts of character traits do you think a person needs in order to grow in God's image? (For starters, see Gal. 5:22-23.)

- In what ways do you think we Western Christians might tend to avoid trials?

- Have you had the privilege of knowing a Christian who was truly wise? Share one or two examples of the wise counsel you have received from such a person.

- What is God saying to *you* in James 1:9-11? Are you one who needs to take pride in your high position or in your low position? Explain.

- In what ways is God directing you toward a mature faith or Christian character? Share an example of the joy you experience in your life as a Christian.

Goalsetting (5 minutes)

As you begin this study of James, you may wish to set a goal of praying for God's guidance in living wisely and joyfully for Jesus, whatever times may come. Ask for the strength to remember God in times of blessing and to keep trusting God in times of struggle.

Closing (5-10 minutes)

Preparing for Prayer—This is a time for sharing praise items and concerns that you'd like the others in your group to bring before God in prayer for you, both now and during the coming week. You may also want to ask for prayers for God's help in meeting the goal you've set during this session.

Prayer—Close your session with prayer, asking the Lord to help you persevere joyfully in times of struggle and to live wisely for Jesus' sake always. Everyone may join in with prayer concerns and praises. Then ask for continued blessing and guidance in the coming weeks as you study the book of James together.

Before parting till your next meeting, you may want to read together from Psalm 46, which reminds us that "God is our refuge and strength, an ever-present help in trouble" (46:1). You could also sing a parting song, such as "Go Now in Peace" or "Lord, Dismiss Us with Your Blessing."

When tempted,
what's a
Christian
to do?

2

JAMES 1:13-27

Temptation and Discipline

In a Nutshell

In times of trial, or testing, we can be intensely tempted. That's why we're called to draw deeply on the godly wisdom, faith, and new life reserved for us in Christ, as we discussed in lesson 1. All these good gifts, along with "pure joy" (James 1:2) and more, are available from God our Father (1:17), who urges us to practice disciplines that can steel us against temptations and help us persevere on the path to Christian maturity.

James 1:13-27

13When tempted, no one should say, "God is tempting me." For God cannot be tempted by evil, nor does he tempt anyone; 14but each one is tempted when, by his own evil desire, he is dragged away and enticed. 15Then, after desire has conceived, it gives birth to sin; and sin, when it is full-grown, gives birth to death.

16Don't be deceived, my dear brothers. 17Every good and perfect gift is from above, coming down from the Father of the heavenly lights, who does not change like shifting shadows. 18He chose to give us birth through the word of truth, that we might be a kind of firstfruits of all he created.

19My dear brothers, take note of this: Everyone should be quick to listen, slow to speak and slow to become angry, 20for man's anger does not bring about the righteous life that God desires. 21Therefore, get rid of all moral filth and the evil that is so prevalent and humbly accept the word planted in you, which can save you.

22Do not merely listen to the word, and so deceive yourselves. Do what it says. 23Anyone who listens to the word but does not do what it says is like a man who looks at his face in a mirror 24and, after looking at himself, goes away and immediately forgets what he looks like. 25But the man who looks intently into the perfect law that gives freedom, and continues to do this, not forgetting what he has heard, but doing it—he will be blessed in what he does.

26If anyone considers himself religious and yet does not keep a tight rein on his tongue, he deceives himself and his religion is worthless. 27Religion that God our Father accepts as pure and faultless is this: to look after orphans and widows in their distress and to keep oneself from being polluted by the world.

The Real Evil

In lesson 1 we focused on many positive things to draw strength from in tough times. We looked at joy, wisdom, faith, and new life in Christ. We talked of blessing and hope in God's promises. But, as we also noted, we may not gloss over the negative elements we have to face in times of struggle. We may not deny the reality or the pain of suffering just because we know God can use it to shape our lives toward faith and blessing.

What are we to think of these troublesome and even terrifying aspects of life in this broken world? What are we to make of the temptations that can bombard us in trying times? Is God responsible for the evil or the temptation? James answers this real problem with a resounding no (1:13). The evil of a trial is not primarily or even necessarily in its discomfort (such as distress, pain, confusion, loneliness, or other suffering). The real evil is in a person's choice to do wrong when he or she is tempted.

The real evil is not that I hurt. Hurt can be beneficial, causing me to pull my hand from a flame. Even great hurt can work to my ultimate benefit. The real evil is in my choice to distance myself from God, to set aside the yoke of my Savior and go in other directions, when I am tempted in times of struggle. This is the true temptation in hard times: that I trust God less and love my neighbor less.

The God of the Bible does not provide the gateway to weakened trust and love. God does not in any way direct us to evil. The reason for this, says James, is that the greatness of God's own character cannot be penetrated by evil. God is fully holy, completely pure, and entirely unlike anything we have experienced. God is untouchable by evil. Evil can have no part of God. And evil can have no part of any of God's actions.

The Real Danger

So where does the evil of hard times come from? James says real evil begins with the evil desires of the human heart (1:14). James clearly teaches that the source of evil is our own self. Here James is closely following the teaching of Jesus (Matt. 15:10-20). Not all desire is evil, of course. God created our desires along with the rest of our being. But evil desire can entice and pull so as to drag away. An evil desire that is kept around, pampered, and played with will eventually drag us away from God and turn us to sin.

And sin that is permitted, not dealt with, not faced for what it truly is, "gives birth to death" (James 1:15). In other words, sin results in death. Again James is describing a process. Sinning is not just breaking a rule; it's striking out on our own path and rejecting God. And walking away from God is not just allowing our pet desires to guide us; it is chasing death. Eventually it breeds eternal death, but it is always shadowing personal and spiritual death.

The real danger in hard times does not come from God. The real danger comes from our own evil desires, which can turn into sin and death. The clear truth we must declare is that *every good* and *only good* comes from the God who has sent our Savior, Jesus Christ. From James 1:16-17 we can surmise that early Christians may well have been beset by many false teachings about the source of good. James declares that if something is good, it must be from God (1:17). And in this context about trials and God's purpose for our lives, we can see that James is not first of all referring to the more material or lesser "goods" of our lives. James is pointing us to what is truly good and right, even "perfect" (1:4), in human living.

The Real Life

James points to God the Father as the source of all the powers and mysteries of creation along with "every good and perfect gift" (1:17). God alone is the one we can trust through all times and events. There is no shifting like shadows in the character or purposes of God.

God's purpose for us is clearly to give life. Real life comes to us as we encounter "the word of truth" (1:18), the good news brought by the eternal Word, who became flesh and died for human sin, who rose again to give eternal life to all who trust in him. And God's purpose in giving life to us is that we, as "firstfruits," might represent the promise of a great harvest of more believers, and even be used by God in bringing life to "all he created" (1:18).

God does not bring evil to us in our trials and struggles; God brings closer to us the honor of promising and bringing life—eternal, hopeful, purposeful life—to all creation.

Disciplines

James next urges us to practice disciplines that will help bring about and prove the Word's growing effect in our lives. He directs us to be careful in the way we handle anger, to listen, to be careful in our speech, and to be active in doing as the Word says (1:19).

Handling Anger

A popular trend in recent years is to note that our feelings are part of who we are as created by God. Modern wisdom also tells us that feelings we hold inside us, or feelings we deny having, eventually cause behavior that's destructive to our well-being. One result of this modern wisdom is that people who used to be called short-tempered are now often referred to as "straightforward." For many Christians today, anger is excused as part of the creation order or as an unavoidable inheritance from parents.

James would not argue with the idea that anger is a God-given feeling like any other—and is therefore not necessarily bad. But James is careful to point out that what leads to anger and what we do with anger can make a difference in becoming the people God wants us to be. It seems that James mentions anger here because it can often be an outgrowth of human pride and can keep believers from hearing God's words to them. Anger is usually a feeling associated with personal injury. Anger says, "I am threatened, and I don't deserve it!" Anger is a tool God gives us to help us deal with hurt. But when controlled only by our personal pride and fear, anger can become a means to hide ourselves and to hurt others.

James points out that we are wrong if we think our own prideful anger will help advance God's cause in us or in the world (1:20). James also implies that in many cases our own moral weakness may be behind our anger (1:21). Human anger serves the important function of pointing out hurts that have happened. In other words, it's often the indicator of a deeper emotion—namely, hurt. And the hurt beneath our anger can be the result of some personal weakness. But anger that is savored or freely expressed can be at least as harmful as anger that is denied. So, rather than merely spouting off our anger, says James, we, as Christians, may need to face up to the personal weakness that may have contributed to the hurt behind the anger.

Listening

Another discipline James mentions is the importance of listening. If indeed God's Word of salvation will heal the hurt behind our anger, we must listen to that Word.

In James's day, the Word of the gospel was not yet widely distributed in written form. To grow in faith, people had to listen. They needed to develop acute skills for listening to each other. God's plan for shaping and re-forming lives was proceeding as people listened to believers who already knew the good news of Jesus. God's people needed to hear and find joy in the Lord's direction for their living.

Today we believers must still listen for the good news in the words of our brothers and sisters. The availability of the written (and printed) Word of God has not taken away the truth that God's Spirit interprets and applies the good news through our active listening to one another in Christ.

Speaking Carefully
The importance of listening is closely related to the importance of careful speaking. For example, if people are listening to me to hear God speaking, I'd better be careful about what I say.

I remember talking at length to someone once and noticing that he was not listening to me. As I continued, I started stringing words together that made no sense. I said something about boats flying up a building until the horses could chop purple clouds in cube roots. My listener eventually noticed and said, "What did you say?" I responded by saying, truthfully, "Nothing much." When we understand that the growth of faith and obedience—and, as a result, blessing and joy—can depend on our speaking God's words in line with the Spirit's desire to work in people's hearts, we'll be careful in our speech.

Doing
To advance God's cause, we Christians must also do more than speak godly words and listen. We also must do as the Word says. We deceive ourselves if we think it's enough merely to listen (1:22). To accent the ridiculous nature of our deception, James compares it to looking in a mirror and then forgetting what we have seen (1:23-24). The point of this illustration is that a mirror shows us what we need to correct. How very foolish for a person to see in a mirror what ought to be done and then to walk away and do nothing about it. The mirror in this passage is a symbol of the gospel, "the word planted in you" (1:21), "the perfect law that gives freedom" (1:25), by which God evidently intends to nurture us continually. As we come to know God—God's grace, God's will, God's blessing—as presented in the gospel, we also come to know ourselves. We begin to see not only our weaknesses and sins but also our victories and growth in Jesus.

The main point is that God's blessing (completeness, maturity, joy) comes to believers who do as they hear God's Word directing them to do (1:25). Christians must control what they say. Anyone who thinks he or she is religious and yet speaks whatever comes to mind is living a lie. Such religion is worthless (1:26), for it does not influence a person to speak according to the pattern of God's will as seen in Christ.

Now, if such religion is worthless, what does God want? It's interesting that James quickly turns here not to carefully crafted theological figures of speech but to simple action. James directs us to help the weak in society ("orphans and widows") and to stay away from the motives and actions of "the world" outside of Christ (1:27). Here James seems to be saying that actions speak louder than words. God's blessing of maturity in Christ gives us comfort and courage. And our living out of God's character of love will call others to have comfort, courage, and trust in our Lord.

The disciplines James recommends for hard times call to every believer in every age: listen for God's Word; speak as God's own child; show by your actions that you are living for the God of grace.

Additional Notes

1:14—James says that temptations come from within. But where does Satan fit in? Isn't he the one behind our temptations, as he was behind the temptations of Adam and Eve (Gen. 3) and Jesus (Matt. 4:1-11)? James does not ignore the devil, for later he writes that "envy and selfish ambition" are "of the devil" (James 3:14-15) and that we must "resist the devil" as we submit ourselves to God (4:7). Satan whispers his temptations to our hearts, and if he gains a hearing, our own evil desires can lead us to sin. (See also Jesus' teaching in Mark 7:14-23.)

1:15—James agrees thoroughly with the apostle Paul that "the wages of sin is death" (Rom. 6:23).

1:18—How does a person become a Christian? Somewhere in the process, the *true Word of God* must be spoken. We can speak of a silent witness to Jesus (such as a cup of cold water or a bowl of hot soup), but no one becomes a believer unless he or she hears the message of salvation in the name of Jesus. Every Christian should be able, however briefly, to explain the message of God's good news of salvation in the name of Jesus and lead a person to a faith commitment.

1:21—The Greek word here for "get rid of" is the word used for taking off clothes. The apostle Paul uses the metaphor of taking off and putting on clothes as a picture of getting rid of our sinful nature and replacing it with the new life made possible in Christ (see Eph. 4:22-24; Col. 3:9-10, 12-14).

1:25—As in 1:12, James delivers a beatitude, which could read like this: "Blessed are those who look into the perfect law and shape their lives accordingly." Note also the parallel in this passage to Jesus' parable of the wise and foolish builders—about hearing and doing the Word of God (Matt. 7:24-27).

1:26—As we discuss James 3:1-12 in lesson 5, we'll focus more closely on sins of the tongue and how our tongues can easily get us into trouble.

1:27—In the ancient world, "widows and orphans" were the two main categories of people who had no one to stand up for them to plead their cause. Neither women nor children had any legal standing in courts of law, so it was easy for unscrupulous people to take advantage of them (see 2 Kings 4:1-7; Luke 20:47). The Greek word for "look after" means "care for" (the same Greek root is also used in Matt. 25:36, 43).

GENERAL DISCUSSION

1. List two or three examples of sin and explain how these sins develop by way of desire. How can we tell the difference between a good desire and an evil one?

2. When, if ever, have you felt that God was responsible for evil in your life? What was the greatest danger to you at such a time?

3. Think of one or two things that tend to make you angry. What does this say about what's important to you? Under what circumstances is "righteous anger" acceptable?

4. "Think before you speak" is a motto James would agree with. But what do you suppose God wants us to think before we speak?

5. What does James 1:27 say to you? What does James mean by "pure and faultless" religion?

SMALL GROUP SESSION IDEAS

Opening (10-15 minutes)
Pray/Worship—As you open this session with prayer, begin by praising the Lord as the "compassionate and gracious God, slow to anger, abounding in love and faithfulness" (Ex. 34:6). Ask for God's wisdom and guidance as you discuss the material for this lesson, and pray that you may have open hearts not only to listen to God's Word but also to do what it says.

If your group likes to sing, a fitting song as you open this session would be "Christian, Do You Struggle" or "What a Friend We Have in Jesus." If you'd like to read an appropriate psalm passage, try Psalm 119:1-16 or Psalm 103.

Share—If any newcomers have joined your group, allow time for introductions before sharing with each other how you're doing so far on this study of James. You may also want to comment on goals you may have set at the end of session 1.

Focus—Throughout this session try to keep in mind the following focus question: *How do I handle temptation, and what can I do in God's strength to deal with it?*

Growing (35-40 minutes)
Read (optional)—You may wish to read the Scripture passage and review portions of the lesson notes before moving into your discussion time.

Discuss—In addition to the General Discussion questions, you may want to discuss some of the following process questions:

* Think of a time when you heard God's Word of blessing from a Christian sister or brother. In what ways did that affect you in comparison with times when you may have been spoken to in anger?

- When do you least expect what you hear from another Christian to be God's Word for you?

- Think of one or two examples of listening to and doing God's Word. In what ways do examples like these confirm what James teaches in the passage for this lesson?

Goalsetting (5 minutes)

Try working on one of the following goals, or one of your own design, as a result of this lesson:

- I need God's help in dealing with temptations. Along with asking God to help me trust that I won't be tempted or tested beyond what I can bear (1 Cor. 10:13), I want to commit to living purely and being "a kind of firstfruits" for my Creator and Savior (James 1:18).

- I need God's help in dealing with anger. I want to be like the Lord, who is "slow to anger" (Ex. 34:6), and I want to learn how to avoid sinning when I do become angry.

Closing (10-15 minutes)

Preparing for Prayer—As you prepare to close, take some time to share joys and concerns that you'd like others to bring before the Lord for you, both now and in the coming week.

Prayer—If you haven't already read Psalm 103 during this session, you could do so now as you begin your prayer. Everyone may join in with joys and concerns that have been mentioned. Ask God again to help each one of you not only to listen to the Word but also to obey in your everyday living.

Group Project (Optional)

Some or all of you may be interested in learning more about some of the topics that have come up in this session. Local Christian bookstores and libraries may be able to help with resources on dealing with temptation, effective listening and speaking, anger, abuse, and the problem of evil. For a few resources that can help you get started, we recommend the following:

- *Not the Way It's Supposed to Be: A Breviary of Sin* (Grand Rapids, Mich.: Eerdmans, 1995) by Cornelius Plantinga, Jr.

- *Handbook of Christian Apologetics* (Downers Grove, Ill.: InterVarsity, 1994) by Peter Kreeft and Ronald K. Tacelli

- *The Enigma of Anger: Essays on a Sometimes Deadly Sin* (San Francisco: Jossey-Bass, 2002) by Garret Keizer
- *Exploring Your Anger: Friend or Foe?* (Grand Rapids, Mich.: Baker/Revell, 1997) by Glenn Taylor and Rod Wilson
- *Preventing Child Abuse: A Guide for Churches* (Grand Rapids, Mich.: Faith Alive, 1997) by Beth Swagman
- *Responding to Domestic Violence: A Resource for Church Leaders* (Grand Rapids, Mich.: Faith Alive, 2002) by Beth Swagman

*Does a
Christian play
favorites?*

3

JAMES 2:1-13

Favoritism Versus Freedom

In a Nutshell

James wants his readers, as believers in Christ, to know that favoritism can be a serious block to becoming mature in faith. Favoritism, or prejudice, simply does not fit with complete Christian living.

In our passage for this lesson James implies that people who favor the rich and trust in riches oppose the work of Jesus Christ in this world. By extension this means that believers who favor the "well off" of the world can be supporters of people, ideas, and institutions that oppose Christ. To remind us about living God's way, James focuses on the Christian's relationship to God's law, which gives freedom.

James 2:1-13

¹My brothers, as believers in our glorious Lord Jesus Christ, don't show favoritism. ²Suppose a man comes into your meeting wearing a gold ring and fine clothes, and a poor man in shabby clothes also comes in. ³If you show special attention to the man wearing fine clothes and say, "Here's a good seat for you," but say to the poor man, "You stand there" or "Sit on the floor by my feet," ⁴have you not discriminated among yourselves and become judges with evil thoughts?

⁵Listen, my dear brothers: Has not God chosen those who are poor in the eyes of the world to be rich in faith and to inherit the kingdom he promised those who love him? ⁶But you have insulted the poor. Is it not the rich who are exploiting you? Are they not the ones who are dragging you into court? ⁷Are they not the ones who are slandering the noble name of him to whom you belong?

⁸If you really keep the royal law found in Scripture, "Love your neighbor as yourself," you are doing right. ⁹But if you show favoritism, you sin and are convicted by the law as lawbreakers. ¹⁰For whoever keeps the whole law and yet stumbles at just one point is guilty of breaking all of it. ¹¹For he who said, "Do not commit adultery," also said, "Do not murder." If you do not commit adultery but do commit murder, you have become a lawbreaker.

¹²Speak and act as those who are going to be judged by the law that gives freedom, ¹³because judgment without mercy will be shown to anyone who has not been merciful. Mercy triumphs over judgment!

Avoiding Favoritism

Let's review the development of ideas we have seen so far in James's letter. God's promise to the Christian is that true maturity waits on the other side of trial (James 1:2-5, 12). Passing through trial to maturity calls for listening to the full message of God's Word and doing as we hear. That's because perseverance in passing through trials involves a lot more than just surviving them; it involves a deepening trust in Christ and obedience to God's ways. The Word of God calls believers to trust in the Lord and to give of themselves to help people who are weak and helpless. So a further discipline we need on the way toward maturity is to avoid catering to the rich and powerful, the favored ones, of this world.

James says that the memory of who Jesus is and what he has done should move believers away from favoritism (2:1). At the center of the Christian faith is the reality that Jesus, who is and always has been fully divine, became a servant. Along with this reality is the truth that Jesus consistently stood on the side of the poor and weak, no matter what type of people he was with. Jesus reached out to all, but he gave special attention to blind, lame, rejected, and otherwise disadvantaged people.

James calls his readers to reawaken in their hearts the true character of the wondrous Lord they learned to trust in. The result of this reawakening ought to destroy favoritism in the Christian heart. The example of favoritism that James gives next—that of the rich and poor being ushered to vastly different seats (2:2-3)—may seem a bit extreme. But James's illustration may well be based on an incident or practice that was reported to him (see Additional Notes on 2:1). And we have to admit that (perhaps less overt) variations of this example happen all the time in worldly society, which usually favors money and power over concern for the poor.

Two Bad Results

James points out two bad results of believers' prejudging people and favoring some people over others (2:4). The first is that believers who do these things become discriminating in their relationships. In some ways, being a discriminating Christian is good. Christians need to be able to make careful distinctions and choose between right and wrong; careful and decisive choices are a mark of maturity. But as discerning believers, we must avoid discriminating in terms of external factors that our society tends to hold in high regard or, conversely, in low esteem.

The second bad result is that believers who show favoritism and prejudice allow evil standards to become the basis for making judgments. James hints here at an illustration of a judge who accepts bribes rather than upholding the law. The pattern seems to be that once we have used corrupt standards for judging or choosing our friends (favorites), we will gradually let those standards shape more and more of our decisions—and eventually all our decision making will be based on corrupt thinking.

The Measure of Money

James points out forcefully how we can invite problems by allowing money to be a standard for Christian judgment (2:5-7). When we explore God's Word, we meet the God who has selected the rejects of this world to have true riches (2:5). Again and again in Scripture we see God blessing those who have been overlooked, passed by, forcibly rejected. And what God gives is not necessarily what would bring these people into favored status in the world's eyes. God gives faith: the ability to trust fully and, as a result, to be free and to truly live. God also gives the kingdom: a place full of hope that offers a way of living in pure joy after God's own heart.

We must avoid insulting the poor, the rejected, the passed-by people of this world—especially those in our own community (2:6). God blesses and is on the side of such people. James warns that people who are financially secure are often the ones who have resisted the claims of Christ and the church. It seems that Jesus is often seen as a threat to the world's ideas of security and status. That may be why James speaks so forcefully about the actions of rich people (2:6-7).

Though we can assume that some of the rich people James is referring to are Christians, it may be hard to understand how they could "slander the noble name" of Jesus (2:7). But people can commit slander in their actions as well as in their words. When Christians act as if money is the first and deciding factor in their judgments, when they speak as if security and happiness can be found mainly in terms of the money a person has, when they behave toward others as if the world's values are right and true, then the message of the servant Christ and the meaning of his name are slandered.

The Royal Law

James refers to the "royal law found in Scripture" as the standard for persons to do what is "right" (2:8). Pointing out that "Love your neighbor as yourself" (Lev. 19:18) summarizes all of the expressed will of God, James is recalling the clear teaching of Jesus that there is much more to obeying God's will than a slavish adherence to the rules of the law (see Matt. 22:34-40). God's will is that we live by the spirit of the law, the spirit of love we are shown in Christ (John 15:9-17). God wants us to show full and free love to all people, as Jesus did.

God's law is indeed "royal," for it is the Word of the King of righteousness, the Anointed One (Messiah) who is Lord of all things. Some early Jewish rabbis had used the term "royal law" in their teaching as well. The law of God is the will of God, and only the Lord Jesus has fulfilled that will perfectly, paving the way for us to follow. To walk truly in God's will, then, we must walk in the way of Jesus. And what is the way of Jesus? What is the law of God as Jesus would have us live by it? If we truly follow the royal law of our true King, then we do what is right. We love our neighbor as a result of loving the Lord our God with all our heart, soul, mind, and strength (see Mark 12:30-31).

Breaking the Law

When I was a child, I heard the words "Love your neighbor as yourself" every Sunday. But during the school week I made various observations about the two other boys my age who lived on my street. One was a great ballplayer and a smart student. The other was less than good on the ball field and a lot less than good in the classroom. The former had sharp clothes and told good jokes. The latter was sloppy and was sometimes a real bore. Guess which one I made plans to play with? Guess which one I avoided, even hid from, on many sunny afternoons? It wasn't until later that I began to understand what I had done.

Several years later I overheard some classmates talking about me in the coatroom at school. They laughed. They told jokes about my clothes, my voice, my mannerisms. It was as if someone were tightening a noose around my neck. Something inside me died that day. It was the same thing I had tortured and strangled in the "lesser" boy who had lived near me.

James warns all Christians that showing favoritism places us under the judgment of God's law (2:9). The argument here is based on two ideas. First, we must consider the law a whole unit; it cannot be divided. Anyone who breaks "a piece" of the law has broken all of it (2:10). We need to see the will of God as one vast design, and if we reconstruct any section, we change the shape of the whole. To violate some part of God's will is to cast doubt and disobedience across the entire pattern.

Second, James strongly implies that favoritism is a form of murder. Adultery was clearly a violation of God's revealed law, and the Jewish Christians to whom James wrote very likely avoided that sin carefully—at least in their outward actions (2:11; see Matt. 5:28). They also would have avoided killing anyone. But James makes a connection in 2:11 between favoritism and murder. He is following the teaching of Jesus that murder is more than physically ending another person's life. Murder also exists clearly in anger and hatred (Matt. 5:21-24). And our Lord clearly wants us to help and show compassion to "the least" of the people around us (see Matt. 25:31-46). If we fail to do that, we fail to love our neighbors as ourselves, and that lack of love is murderous.

When we show favoritism, we favor one person over another, practicing at least a neglect but more commonly a downright lack of love for the "lesser" one. Our King gave himself in love for the unlovely. The actions of those claimed by the love of Jesus should reveal a desire to lift up the disadvantaged and thus work at fulfilling God's will.

Bringing Freedom

James next encourages his readers to "speak and act" according to the standard of "the law that gives freedom" (2:12). Here again James uses a phrase that Jewish teachers historically used ("the law that gives freedom"). And since Jesus, the Messiah, had come and had fulfilled that law perfectly, the freedom and blessing of God's law were now fully available to all who believed in him.

The only source of freedom for people is the grace of God that comes through faith in Jesus Christ. Grace, God's mercy toward sinners who do not deserve it, expresses most fully the will of God. The unmerited mercy of God brings freedom, and this mercy, clearly revealed in the person and work of Jesus, reveals the heart of God's law as our guide for living. James calls all believers to "speak and act" according to the standard of God's mercy (2:13). True human freedom comes when we live by this standard in the strength of the Holy Spirit of God.

Judged by Our Own Standards

James also warns that when we set up standards for judging, those standards will be applied to us also (2:13). (The apostle Paul develops this same theme in Romans 2:1-11.)

People show how much they know about right and wrong by what they expect of others. The standards of fairness that we want others to follow, especially in their dealings with us, are often closer to God's will than the standards we actually follow. James takes this line of reasoning a step further: we do not want to be finally judged according to God's perfect justice. (Paul also follows this line of thought throughout the rest of his letter to the Romans.) If we insist that a standard of rules or values be placed on everyone, and that each person be treated according to that standard to ensure fairness, then we place ourselves under the final scrutiny of God's perfect standard—which we cannot measure up to. James is urging believers, therefore, to always remember that their only hope rests on mercy, not on personal ability, to meet the standard of righteousness God requires. Mercy has triumphed over judgment (2:13)!

In Christ we are not judged and found wanting, and we're certainly not prejudged (Rom. 8:1-4). The Christian is a person whose life is being overwhelmed and filled by perfect mercy. If such a person is truly coming alive, truly maturing in trust, he or she will show mercy more and more in the decisions of everyday living. For such a person, there is no place for pre-judging, favoritism, or judging by the world's standards.

Facing life's trials with joy is intimately connected with how much favoritism and prejudice we let into our hearts. The trust in our Lord that brings life and joy cannot be separated from the way we relate to those around us, whether rich or poor.

Additional Notes

2:1—From the Greek sentence structure we can tell that James is speaking here of a practice that is actually taking place among his first readers. The original Greek text literally reads, "Do not keep showing favoritism" or "Stop showing favoritism." Note also 2:6: "You *have* insulted the poor."

2:2—The Greek word for "shabby" is related to the word for "moral filth" in 1:21. Perhaps a better translation for "shabby" would be "filthy." In other words, the person described is not only poor but is also sloppy and dirty—someone whose appearance might disgust a clean and neat person.

2:5—Even though James is critical of his readers, he loves them deeply, calling them "dear" ("beloved," NRSV).

2:8—The apostle Paul also wrote that "Love your neighbor as yourself" summarizes God's law (see Rom. 13:8-10).

2:10-11—James is not suggesting that it's possible to keep the whole law except for one tiny aspect. Note 3:2, where he writes that "we all stumble in many ways."

2:13—Jesus told a parable about a servant who was released from a debt but who would not release another person from a debt owed to him. His point was that those who have received forgiving mercy from God should show mercy in their relations with others; otherwise they are in danger of losing God's mercy themselves (see Matt. 18:23-35). If you have time, you may want to read this parable and discuss it briefly together.

GENERAL DISCUSSION

1. What sorts of people are most likely to be your favorites? What sorts of people are least likely to receive "favors" in your community of faith?

2. In what ways do we tend to use money as a standard for decision making in our Christian community today? How might this be dangerous?

3. How might we slander Jesus' name, either by words or by actions?

4. James states that we can break the whole law by breaking just one part of it. He also says, "If you keep the royal law found in Scripture . . . you are doing right" (2:8). How are the parts of the law interrelated, and what difference is there between the whole law and "the royal law"?

5. How does God's mercy bring us freedom? How does our showing mercy bring freedom?

6. What prejudices are most difficult for you to be rid of? Why should you work to be rid of them?

SMALL GROUP SESSION IDEAS

Opening (10-15 minutes)

Pray—Open with prayer, asking the Holy Spirit to help you individually and as a group to identify and uproot practices of favoritism and prejudice so that you may grow in Christian freedom.

If you like singing, a song of confession and assurance, such as "Lord, I Want to Be a Christian" or "God, Be Merciful to Me" can help set an appropriate tone for this session.

Share—Share with each other how things are going with this study of James or with particular goals or projects you've committed to.

Focus—Throughout this session keep in mind the following question: *What favoritism or prejudice do I struggle with, and what can I do about it?*

Growing (35-40 minutes)

Read (optional)—You may wish to read James 2:1-13 and portions of the lesson notes before moving into your discussion time.

Discuss—In addition to the General Discussion questions, include some or all of the following process questions wherever they might fit in your discussion:

- Reflect on and share your thoughts about the following statement: "When a man tells you that he got rich through hard work, ask him, 'Whose?'" (Don Marquis, columnist).

- Have you ever had to admonish someone who was showing favoritism? If so, what did you say? How did the person respond?

- Think about how you might explain the difference between favoritism and Christian freedom to someone who isn't a believer in Christ. What would you say?

- Has anyone ever had a reason to say to you, "How can you do that and call yourself a Christian?" What does that make you think about living for Christ and honoring his name?

Goalsetting (5 minutes)

Try working on the following goal, or one of your own design, as a result of this lesson:

- I need God's help in dealing with favoritism and really living in Christian freedom. Here's what I want to ask God to help me do:

Closing (10-15 minutes)

Preparing for Prayer—Share joys or concerns you'd like to include in the closing prayer for this session.

Prayer—Ask for God's wisdom and guidance in dealing with any issues in your lives that may have emerged during this session. Everyone may join in with personal prayer requests. Also ask that we may all root out favoritism and prejudice in any aspects of our lives and embrace the freedom of living God's way, as Jesus showed by his example.

Group Project (Optional)

Some or all of you may sense the Spirit's call to work against prejudice and discrimination in our society, in the workplace, in your church or neighborhood or personal life, or elsewhere. Libraries, Christian bookstores, denominational agencies, and parachurch ministries can help you gather information, resources, and ideas to get started. We recommend the following resources and contacts:

- *More Than Equals: Racial Healing for the Sake of the Gospel* (Downers Grove, Ill.: InterVarsity, 2000) by Spencer Perkins and Chris Rice.

- *Churches That Make a Difference: Reaching Your Community with Good News and Good Works* (Grand Rapids, Mich.: Baker, 2002) by Ronald J. Sider, et al.

- *A Covenant to Keep: Biblical Meditations on the Theme of Justice* (Grand Rapids, Mich.: CRC Publications, 2000) by James W. Skillen

- Office of Race Relations, Office of Social Justice and Hunger Action, Office of Abuse Prevention (Christian Reformed Church); visit *www.crcna.org* or call 1-800-272-5125.

*Is faith without
deeds even
faith at all?*

4

JAMES 2:14-26

Gracious Goodness

In a Nutshell

God wants us to show by our actions that our faith is real. In other words, if we say we have faith but we don't show in our daily living that we serve God, our faith is "useless" (James 2:20). Even worse, it is "dead" (2:17, 26). Just as we know we are not saved by works but by grace alone through faith (Eph. 2:8), we can also know that our faith is real by the good we do, being made new in Christ (2 Cor. 5:17; Eph. 2:10).

James 2:14-26

¹⁴What good is it, my brothers, if a man claims to have faith but has no deeds? Can such faith save him? ¹⁵Suppose a brother or sister is without clothes and daily food. ¹⁶If one of you says to him, "Go, I wish you well; keep warm and well fed," but does nothing about his physical needs, what good is it? ¹⁷In the same way, faith by itself, if it is not accompanied by action, is dead.

¹⁸But someone will say, "You have faith; I have deeds."

Show me your faith without deeds, and I will show you my faith by what I do. ¹⁹You believe that there is one God. Good! Even the demons believe that—and shudder.

²⁰You foolish man, do you want evidence that faith without deeds is useless?

²¹Was not our ancestor Abraham considered righteous for what he did when he offered his son Isaac on the altar? ²²You see that his faith and his actions were working together, and his faith was made complete by what he did. ²³And the scripture was fulfilled that says, "Abraham believed God, and it was credited to him as righteousness," and he was called God's friend. ²⁴You see that a person is justified by what he does and not by faith alone.

²⁵In the same way, was not even Rahab the prostitute considered righteous for what she did when she gave lodging to the spies and sent them off in a different direction? ²⁶As the body without the spirit is dead, so faith without deeds is dead.

Practice, Practice

Some years ago I coached a team of young basketball players. When we practiced, they immediately wanted to play a game. I insisted that to play, we had to do drills: run, pass, dribble, jump. They grumbled, but for much of our time together there was no game play—only run, pass, dribble, jump. Later one of those young people, who was now on a high school team, remarked that he was still doing the same stuff. He now realized that while the point of basketball is to get the ball in the hoop and score points, you can't do that without practice: run, pass, dribble, jump.

Are There Two Kinds of Faith?

James explains that in the Christian life we can't have faith without good deeds. In other words, good deeds are not just things we can do to enhance faith; they're the proof that our faith is real. If there is faith, there will be good deeds.

We need to pay careful attention to James's two questions in 2:14. Notice that the hypothetical person in the first question *claims* to have faith. We may not suppose that James is contrasting "faith" and "works" here. He is contrasting two supposed types of faith. One is a "claimed faith" presumed to exist without good works, without the discipline to exercise right actions. The other is a faith that can't help producing good works; by its very nature it inspires discipline toward doing what is right.

James's next question asks whether faith without works can actually save a person. The underlying question here is "How can we tell what true saving faith is?" Certainly we may not think we can have all the information necessary to judge whether a person's faith is valid. But are some elements of true faith outwardly visible in believers' lives? The answer is "Yes, we should see discipline toward good works in their lives." And the answers to James's questions in 2:14 are "No good" and "No," respectively.

No Good, No Faith

James's next example (2:15-17) reinforces this point by portraying a fellow believer who is without basic physical needs. While James's use of "brother or sister" focuses our attention on fellow believers, certainly the teachings of Jesus call us to do good for all people who are in need. James asks, "Now what good is it if a believer wishes a poor person well, even feels pity for him or her, but does nothing about his or her needs?" The obvious answer is "No good." But let's look closely at what this means: faith that is merely full of feeling *does* no good and *is* no good. Such a faith produces no righteousness (good) and is of no value (good) to anyone.

In 2:17 James states clearly, in the negative, that any faith that is true will produce good deeds. The simple truth is that a person cannot truly accept the reality of Jesus Christ—of his birth as the Son of God, his suffering and death, his rising from the dead, and his ascension to the throne of heaven—and not be compelled to action for the sake of God's kingdom. So James is not saying that doing good is a better or higher pathway than faith. He is saying that true faith in Jesus can always be expected to produce good works in our lives. Any other sort of faith is not living but dead and is not a faith in the living Lord, who said he is the "way and the truth and the life" (John 14:6). It's true that Christians will not immediately do every good thing possible when they believe. But neither should the Christian ever be satisfied for long with a faith that is mainly an internal pietism, an emotional fervor, or a private, intellectual matter.

Are There Two Paths?

As James continues, it's as if he can read our minds. Suppose, next, that someone suggests there are actually two paths to Christian maturity and life: one is to have faith, and the other is to do good works. (Presumably the path of works here includes a prerequisite of some degree of faith, since the discussion is about Christian living.) Isn't it true that some people believe in God but just don't seem to be able to make progress in doing what is loving or just or patient or kind or just plain good? And isn't it true that some people seem to be highly productive at doing good things based on their religious attitudes? Taking this a step further, can't we appeal to the concept of spiritual gifts and recognize a difference between the gift of faith and the gifts of doing good (mercy, kindness, healing, hospitality, and so on)? (See 1 Cor. 12-14; Eph. 4:11-13; 1 Pet. 4:10-11.)

No, says James. Faith that does not show is no faith at all (James 2:18), just as love that does not give evidence of loving actions is no love at all. James points out that to believe in God is not the same as to live with God. Living with God demands a faith that is true, a faith that can be seen in what a person does. True faith can be seen in a person's actions because it has claimed the most basic trust in that person's life.

Even beings who are actively opposed to God's ways (such as demons) believe there is one true God (2:19). They accept the existence of God, but they don't live with God and they don't want to. James is saying here that the only way to have a life worth living is to live it with God, in God's ways, in the example of Jesus Christ. A faith that does not live in God's ways is dead.

James reinforces this vital point by bringing up the example of Abraham, the "father of all believers" (2:21-24). We must see James's point here as summarized in 2:22. Abraham did not have a faith that was merely internal, intellectual, or emotional. He was willing to do what God wanted done in the world. And this willingness to take right action was seen as righteousness by God, because his actions were evidence of a true trust in God (Gen. 15:6; 22:15-18; James 2:23). Abraham had a faith that lived and breathed the ways of God. Abraham was considered righteous through a faith that he lived out in good works in obedience to God. No one is justified before God through a faith (belief) that is content to be only an internal, personal matter (2:24).

And in case we think of Abraham as more than an ordinary person, in much the same way that we tend to think of other leaders in the faith—such as pastors, elders, and church school teachers—James also mentions the faith example of Rahab (2:25). This Gentile woman, whom he calls "the prostitute," was saved from the destruction of Jericho and became a part of Israel and even an ancestor of our Lord Jesus (Josh. 2; 6:24-25; Matt. 1:5). James points out that God's blessings to Rahab cannot be seen apart from her actions of good done to the two Israelite spies.

Faith is not one thing for the Christian leader and another for the "average person." Living faith must always be seen in the actions of the believer. That's why maturing faith is the proper goal of every life. Faith is the very substance of who we are and what we do. A Christian without good works is a corpse; supposed faith, the kind without actions, is dead.

Additional Notes

2:15-16—Note that James's example here is not about how the believers treat strangers or visitors but how they treat fellow church members. Concern for the needy begins with the household of faith (see Gal. 6:10).

2:18—A challenge arises in translating this verse because it can be hard to figure out where to put the quotation marks (the original Greek text did not include punctuation). Some translations render the entire verse as a quotation, but the way the New International Version has it seems better. The hypothetical person who speaks here may in fact be distinguishing between spiritual gifts, as if to say, "What's the big deal? You have the gift of faith and I have the gift of deeds. We're each doing what we can with what God has given us."

James, however, clarifies that when one talks about *saving faith*, it is not a question of having one gift or another but of having faith in the Lord Jesus and a desire to serve according to God's will.

2:19—The principle that there is only one God is one of the basic principles of Judaism, confessed every day by Jews even today (based on Deut. 6:4). No wonder the demons know this truth; after all, Satan is well versed in Scripture, as we can see from his temptations of Jesus (Matt. 4:1-11).

2:20—Earlier James said that faith without works is dead (2:17). Here he says it is "useless"—that is, it does not work; it is unproductive.

2:20-24—Note that James does not say God declared Abraham righteous on the basis of his works alone. His faith was critical, and James acknowledges that Abraham's faith was "credited to him as righteousness" (2:21, 23). What was the role of Abraham's works, then? Abraham's actions brought his faith to completeness (2:22), showing that it was real.

2:26—In good rhetorical style, James summarizes the main point he has been making.

GENERAL DISCUSSION

1. What characteristics would you list to describe a truly religious person? *fruits of the spirit*

   wise   loving
   discerning   patient
   helpful
   joyful   kind

2. What is true saving faith? What qualities make our faith "valuable" to God? To what extent may we judge the "value" of a believer's faith according to his or her good works?

   - believing in God & obeying what He commands, loving
   your neighbour which will result in good works
   - being obedient when He asks something of us - good deeds
   - we should not judge anyone else's "good works" it is not
   our place

3. Think of a few ways in which Christians today hide from doing good by ducking behind a shield of faith. Share your answers with your group.

   - saying things like "I'll pray for you" and then not or
   not helping but where they easily could

4. What occupies more of your effort or time, especially in times of trial—matters of faith or of doing good? What sort of faith do you see the trials and challenges of your life producing in you?

SMALL GROUP SESSION IDEAS

Opening (10-15 minutes)

Pray—In your opening prayer, ask for the Spirit's guidance and conviction about faithful living—that is, showing by our actions that our faith in Christ is real. You may also wish to read a psalm that addresses faithful living, such as Psalm 1, or a passage that summarizes God's desire for us, such as Micah 6:8.

Share—Take a few moments to share with each other how things are going with this study or with goals or projects you've committed to.

Focus—Throughout this session try to focus on whether people can tell by the way you speak and act that your faith in Christ is alive. Ask yourself, *In what ways does my faith show? In what ways does it not?*

Growing (35-40 minutes)

Read (optional)—You may wish to read James 2:14-26 together before moving into your discussion time. You may also want to read or review portions of the lesson notes.

Discuss—In addition to the General Discussion questions, include some or all of the following process questions wherever they might fit in your discussion:

- Because our old sinful nature still clings to us even though we are made new in Christ, we sometimes fail to show our faith by our actions. Does this mean our faith is dead or useless? What does this tell us about our own ability to show that our faith is alive? What does this tell us about our dependence on God to work through us each day?
Good deeds should be the result of transforming ya
- Share one or two examples of people you know or know of *not* who have shown real faith in action. Describe the impact *some* their actions have had on you. In what ways have these *we sho* *have to work at,* *just flow natural*

examples helped to strengthen your faith and inspire your
action for God? *Gen - missionary who's given her whole life to serve those in need around the world. George buying new piano for church*

- Think about how you would explain to a nonbeliever what *Holly & Blair babysitting* it means to have real faith, saving faith. Try to keep your *so Naphte & Adam can* explanation in simple terms, and see if you can state it in a *attend Bible study* few brief sentences. *Real faith is security in love & forgiveness that can not be described in words, and this " " causes such a change in you that you can not help but loving the people around you & desiring to do good*

Goalsetting (5 minutes)
Set a goal that has to do with showing your faith more effec-
tively in your daily living. Maybe you need to ask God to help
you identify an area in your life in which you need to be (more)
faithful—and to have the strength to persevere. Commit to
asking for guidance and strength each day and to following
through on your intentions. *Be more eager to be helpful - don't be so cynical towards the realtors. Be more willing to go out of your way*

Closing (10-15 minutes) *to serve John.*
Preparing for Prayer—Share joys or concerns that you'd like to
include in the closing prayer.

Prayer—Thank God for the new life we are given through faith
in Christ, and ask for wisdom and help each day in showing by
our actions that our faith is real. Invite everyone to join in with
personal requests and praises, and perhaps include a time of
silence for personal confession. Claim God's promise of
renewal and vitality of faith, and take up the challenge to show
God's gracious goodness everywhere.

Group Project (Optional)
If you're sensing the Lord's call to put hands and feet to your
faith in ways that you may not have done before, consider
doing a group project based on suggestions at the ends of sessions 2, 3, and 6.

In times of trial,
our words show
the true depth of
our faith.

5

JAMES 3:1-12

What Did You Say?

In a Nutshell

When we speak, we use our powerful potential to build others up and lead them to Christ or to break others down and bring on corruption and suffering. And with our words we deeply affect our own lives for better or for worse. The only way to keep working toward the better is to give our tongues (with our hearts) over to God.

James 3:1-12

¹Not many of you should presume to be teachers, my brothers, because you know that we who teach will be judged more strictly. ²We all stumble in many ways. If anyone is never at fault in what he says, he is a perfect man, able to keep his whole body in check.

³When we put bits into the mouths of horses to make them obey us, we can turn the whole animal. ⁴Or take ships as an example. Although they are so large and are driven by strong winds, they are steered by a very small rudder wherever the pilot wants to go. ⁵Likewise the tongue is a small part of the body, but it makes great boasts. Consider what a great forest is set on fire by a small spark. ⁶The tongue also is a fire, a world of evil among the parts of the body. It corrupts the whole person, sets the whole course of his life on fire, and is itself set on fire by hell.

⁷All kinds of animals, birds, reptiles and creatures of the sea are being tamed and have been tamed by man, ⁸but no man can tame the tongue. It is a restless evil, full of deadly poison.

⁹With the tongue we praise our Lord and Father, and with it we curse men, who have been made in God's likeness. ¹⁰Out of the same mouth come praise and cursing. My brothers, this should not be. ¹¹Can both fresh water and salt water flow from the same spring? ¹²My brothers, can a fig tree bear olives, or a grapevine bear figs? Neither can a salt spring produce fresh water.

Why Are We Doing This?

I was in the grocery store with a half-loaded cart when I began trying to remember what item I had actually gone there for. You may have had a similar experience. You started out on an errand, only to get sidetracked by something, and then you found it hard to remember why you went out in the first place.

Before we go further in this study, let's recall why James is writing. He wants to encourage Christians to have a vibrant, active faith, deepened by the trials they face because of their faith. James's desire is that believers will greet their trials with joy, knowing that faith-testing will help them grow closer to the perfection God wills for them as imagebearers.

Careful Teaching

In chapter 3, James turns our attention to patterns of speech. Still thinking about the hard times we must face as Christians, James makes clear that we should reveal a lively and deeply trusting faith in the way we relate to others by our speech.

It's important to note that James's homily here about our speech flows directly from the idea that Christians are called to teach (3:1). James warns that God will hold accountable believers who presume to instruct others. We should be careful not to instruct others lightly. It often takes longer to unlearn something incorrect than it does to learn correct information.

After all, says James, not one of us perfect. We all have been and will be wrong (3:2). The point is that if we have opportunities to instruct others in the gospel, we ought to approach those situations with great humility and caution. Every Christian should avoid imparting his or her errors to others. A person who teaches becomes responsible in part for what the listener understands to be true. And most teaching takes place outside the classroom, lecture hall, or worship center. When we speak, we put forward our ideas as true, and those who hear and trust us are led by our words. That's why James says teachers will be judged "more strictly" (3:1).

Under Control

At this point James gives examples that show how broadly influential the tongue is. Each of these examples helps to illustrate how controlling our speech can bring other elements of our living under control and in line with God's desires for us.

A bit in a horse's mouth does not affect just the mouth; it allows us to turn the horse's entire body. The horse that was headed in one direction is easily turned in another direction by a firm pull on one side of the bit. Similarly, if you examine your pattern of speaking and you change it, you can turn yourself in a new direction, opening yourself up to new ways of thinking and acting.

It has been some time since I captained a sailboat. And it was a small one. But I will never forget the feel of the rudder as

I tacked upwind. The constant tug of the wind and water against my hand was exhilarating. With a pull of my arm, I could send the boat off on a totally new course, despite the force of the wind and the firm tug of the water. The rudder, though small, controlled the whole ship, despite powerful resisting forces. The tongue of the Christian, when brought consciously under the control of Jesus' love, turns a whole life in the direction of that caring love.

Truly the words of our mouths are small things. But like a bit or a rudder, our little tongues are capable of great power. With God's firm hand to hold them, they can turn the direction of our living from thoughtlessness and selfishness to humility and caring. When James says that the tongue "makes great boasts" (3:5), he is not just saying a small organ can be used to boast about the one who owns it. James is also saying that if the tongue could speak for itself, it could brag of its own powerful accomplishments. Even though words often seem like small, unimportant things, they hold remarkable power to shape even the thinking of the person who speaks them.

Be Careful, Little Tongue

James goes on to warn that often the tongue does not do us good (3:6). Our tongues are often a power to destroy us. The source of any destructive course ("burning") is the evil of hell itself. When we spread stories that are not true and helpful, when we force our opinions on others as the only truth, when we speak in haste with anger, contempt, or bitterness, we set out to destroy the growth of trust and love and Christlikeness in our own lives. This evil is the very laughter of hell itself.

The right control of our speech takes a concerted and disciplined effort, and we cannot do it on our own (3:7-8). Taming the tongue takes time, and the process is tested and proven through trials and challenges in our lives. In times of trial our words reveal the depth of the faith in our hearts. And in such times as we shape our words to Christlikeness, our hearts grow to trust and beat for Christ more and more. So we must never think that what we say is of little importance or consequence. Our words can be the path to "the way and the truth and the life" (John 14:6), or they can offer up more and more evil and death (James 3:8) for ourselves and for others.

It's striking how the words and faith of a believer often contradict each other (3:9). One day he or she will meet with other believers and sing and speak praises to God. Then the next day, by speaking thoughtless words, he or she will heap "curses"

47

(slander, gossip) on fellow human beings, all of whom are God's imagebearers. How utterly inappropriate for a person who knows God's justice (passion for truth) and God's love (passion for mercy) to speak as if neither justice nor love mattered for others.

Not to mention how dangerous! What happens when you add salt water to fresh water (3:11)? Of course, you end up with undrinkable, brackish water. If you mix bad speech with a life moving toward righteousness, that life will be compromised and move back toward destruction. And what would you call a tree that gives pears? An apple tree? (See 3:12.)

Christ expects people who are called Christians to speak in a way that shows the Lord of truth and love lives in them. Our speech is a direct indicator of the condition of our heart.

Additional Notes

3:1—The more responsible our position is in life, the greater is our risk to do damage. Since teaching involves shaping a person's perspective and life, James warns his readers to enter into that task with care. It could be that in James's day many believers were eager for the prestige that came with being a teacher of the faith.

3:7—James apparently has in mind the opening stories in Genesis, which tell of humanity's role as caretaker over the animal world (Gen. 1:28-29; 2:19-20). Our stewardship over creation is ongoing.

3:10—Using the phrase "my brothers," James indicates that the problems with controlling the tongue belong to believers as well as unbelievers.

GENERAL DISCUSSION

1. Which do you think is more important: what we say, how we say it, when we say it, or to whom we say it? Why?

2. List a few ways in which Christians can speak and teach humbly and carefully. Think also of some common results when people speak as if they have all the answers. Share your thoughts with the rest of the group.

3. How is retelling a story third-hand a form of false teaching? Is all gossip malicious? If not, are some forms of gossip less harmful than others? How so?

4. James 3:3-5 talks about the effects of words on people—even on the person who speaks them. How might our lives change for the better if we consciously change our speech patterns?

5. What does James 3:9-10 say about the image of God? Why? How does this teaching relate to the tables of God's law— "Love the Lord your God" and "Love your neighbor"?

SMALL GROUP SESSION IDEAS

Opening (10-15 minutes)

Pray—Open your session with prayer, thanking God for the gift of speech and being made in God's image, and asking for grace and wisdom in the use of our tongues each day.

If your group likes to sing, you may wish to offer praise with a song like "Oh, for a Thousand Tongues," or you could sing "Lord, Speak to Me That I May Speak" as part of your opening prayer.

Share—Share with each other how you're doing on goals or projects you've committed to.

Focus—Keep the following focus question in mind as you work through this session: *In what ways do I show that my tongue is directed by God? In what ways not?*

Growing (35-40 minutes)

Read (optional)—You may wish to read James 3:1-12 together and to read or review portions of the lesson notes.

Discuss—Use the following process questions along with the General Discussion questions.

- Notice the imagery James uses in this section of his letter (the tongue as a bit, a rudder, a spark). Take some time to think about and discuss some other imagery that reminds you of the tongue's power to do good or bad.

- In what ways do you see God speaking to you through the Scripture for this lesson? Share your thoughts with the rest of the group, if you're comfortable doing so.

- Think of one or two ways in which God can (or does) use you as a mouthpiece to bring words of healing, hope, and upbuilding in your church, your group, your community, or elsewhere. Share your thoughts with the rest of the group.

Goalsetting (5 minutes)
I want to commit to the following goal as a result of this lesson:

Closing (10-15 minutes)
Preparing for Prayer—Share joys or concerns that you'd like to include in the closing prayer.

Prayer—Again thank God for the wonderful gift of speech and for the many ways we can use this gift to communicate with each other. Ask especially for God's help in controlling our tongues each day for good, that we may be faithful witnesses for our Lord and Savior. Everyone may join in with additional requests and praises. You may also want to include a time of silence for personal confession. Close with a plea for the Spirit's guidance in all we think, say, and do, especially in the way we treat other imagebearers of God.

True wisdom goes hand in hand with true humility.

6

JAMES 3:13-18

What Kind of Wisdom?

In a Nutshell

In James 3:1-12 we found James focusing on how our speech patterns affect and reflect the inner condition of our hearts (lesson 5). Now, in 3:13-18, James moves into a discussion on the attitudes and directions of the Christian heart. James wants to concentrate on the true wisdom we show by the actions flowing from the inner condition of our heart.

James 3:13-18

13Who is wise and understanding among you? Let him show it by his good life, by deeds done in the humility that comes from wisdom. 14But if you harbor bitter envy and selfish ambition in your hearts, do not boast about it or deny the truth. 15Such "wisdom" does not come down from heaven but is earthly, unspiritual, of the devil. 16For where you have envy and selfish ambition, there you find disorder and every evil practice.

17But the wisdom that comes from heaven is first of all pure; then peace-loving, considerate, submissive, full of mercy and good fruit, impartial and sincere. 18Peacemakers who sow in peace raise a harvest of righteousness.

True Wisdom Marked by Humility

The point of James 3:13 seems to be that if we want to share the true wisdom of Christ, we don't have to be teachers to do so. It's not necessary to be talking all the time to grow in wisdom and to share wisdom. In fact, talking, though necessary for Christian witness and life, has been shown by James to be a dangerous business. If we want to share Christ's true wisdom, suggests James, one of the best ways to do that is by our actions.

James points out that true wisdom, wisdom from God, wisdom of the gospel of Jesus Christ, is marked by true humility. Humility was not highly esteemed in the culture of James's day. It was considered necessary in lower levels of society, but people of "higher" quality believed they didn't need humility.

Humility is not very popular in our culture today either. Christians sing and talk about humility, but they often have real trouble defining and showing it.

No Humility Here . . .

James begins his definition of humility by pointing out that humility is surely not "bitter envy" or "selfish ambition" (3:14). James was aware that in his culture a desire to get ahead (selfish ambition) and to get things or positions that others had (envy) were often matters people would boast about. James further points out that the Christian might piously deny being selfishly ambitious or bitterly envious. But neither boasting nor denial are proper ways of dealing with these vices that cavort around as "wisdom." True wisdom shows itself in actions that clearly demonstrate an inner attitude of humility. The driving attitude behind a self-oriented lifestyle geared to getting ahead is surely not humility. Nor is humility behind the desire to have what others have—or, worse yet, to make sure they can't have it either. Such desires betray an attitude of bitterness, not humility, toward the gifts one already has.

Selfish ambition and envy find their source in this world and in the designs of Satan (3:15). Any attempt to whitewash envy and selfish ambition into positive attitudes is a lie. Doing so may mean "wisdom" to the world and may make sense to the devil, but it's actually a great deception. There is no real joy, wisdom, or comfort in "getting ahead" or in "wanting the good life." In fact, rather than producing good, these attitudes produce disorder and evil practices (3:16).

Actions That Come from Humility

So far James has defined humility in negative terms. Next, in 3:17-18, he describes actions stemming from "the humility that comes from [true] wisdom" (3:13). "First of all," those actions, like the wisdom they come from, are "pure" (3:17). But purity is a rather overwhelming behavior requirement, isn't it? Here James is probably continuing the point that actions moved by humility will clearly not be mixed with or made impure by envy and ambition. The Christian should strive for purity by removing envious and selfish attitudes, which would destroy the very character and growth of humility.

So how do we remove those wrongful attitudes? James says that one thing we need to be is "peace-loving." There can be little peace when we are constantly reacting to deep wounds in our lives. Our wounds need healing if we are to have any peace.

But peace needs to be more than a personal lifestyle of well-being. Being peace-loving means more than just liking it quiet or being pleased when there is no open conflict. People must come together in caring cooperation. It is no chance happening that we can describe Jesus' ministry as one of healing and reconciliation. To be a peace-lover means more than *to like* healing and reconciliation; it means *to desire these things with all our heart and to work toward them*. Such desire and action, under God's direction, leave less and less room in our lives for envy and ambition.

Another thing we need if we are to remove envious and selfish attitudes is to be "considerate." It may help us to understand this quality if we think of *consider* as the root of the word *considerate*. We are to "consider," to think of, others. James is pointing out that if we learn to think of other people's situations, we will handle them with care.

The next item on James's list hits absolute bottom on the scale of human popularity. Along with being peaceloving and considerate, we need to be "submissive." While the word *submit* means basically "to yield to authority," the central meaning for the Christian is "to seek the welfare of others." It's not enough to consider others' hurts and needs and fears. We must move to help others and support them. Humility cannot be real if we are not lifting up those whom we say we love.

Real humility will also seek to show "mercy" to others. Christians who seek God's wisdom at the heart of their lives learn to trust fully in God's mercy. The heart of one who knows God's mercy cannot refer unwaveringly to rules and codes. True wisdom calls us to show mercy after mercy. Our lives must produce an increasing stream of good in the world. Closely connected with mercy, "good fruit" refers to right actions that will inevitably come from a life that feeds on the faithful love of God. People who are in Christ by faith will increasingly desire to show mercy, and more and more good will flow out from them. (The apostle Paul makes a similar point in a discussion of "the fruit of the Spirit" in Galatians 5:16-26. See also Jesus' teaching in John 15:5-8.)

James next returns to two ideas he brought up earlier. We are to be "impartial" and "sincere." Impartiality (2:1-13) and sincerity (1:22-25) are qualities of mind and action that show true godly humility. These, then, are not just nice qualities to have. They are vital parts of the humility that comes from true wisdom.

The Heart of Humility

For James, though, the heart of the humility that develops from true godly wisdom is the deep desire for peace. James now refers not only to peaceloving but also to peacemaking (3:18). This core of God's teaching about wisdom is the seed that produces righteousness (justice). In the mission of peacemaking—that is, healing and reconciling—we find the power that can multiply right deeds.

Our Lord humbled himself and died to make righteousness available to us. Through the wisdom he offers by his example and by his Holy Spirit, we can humble ourselves and bring Jesus' message and work of godly wisdom to a crying world.

Additional Notes

3:13—In James 1:5-6 we have a message about how to get wisdom (to ask and trust God to give it—see lesson 2). Here James is talking about someone who is considered wise. Wisdom is not something merely intellectual, something we can have only in our minds. We will only be considered wise if we show wisdom in our day-to-day living.

3:14—The word for "envy" here is the same word that is often translated elsewhere as "zeal." It's a quality Jesus had when he ran the moneychangers out of the Lord's temple: "Zeal for your house will consume me" (John 2:17). We should all be zealous for the Lord and his work (in 1 Cor. 12:31 the verb for "eagerly desire" derives from the same root as the word for "zeal"). Notice that James qualifies the zeal here as "bitter zeal," or "bitter envy," so that we understand it as the consuming bitterness that comes when we don't get what we want and when we see what someone else has. Obviously such an attitude is nothing to boast about (though we do hear boasting about it, especially in the business world, where it's often called "drive").

3:15-16—It's true, isn't it? In a business, for example, fueled by "envy and selfish ambition," conducted with an attitude of stopping at nothing to get an edge on the competition, we can find "every evil practice." There will also often be dissatisfaction among the employees (who don't share in much of the owner's success but may be pushed to the limit) and therefore "disorder." Such pursuit of earthly values and goals can hardly be said to come "from heaven"; rather, they are "of the devil." Note that it was precisely envy and selfish ambition with which the serpent tempted Eve (Gen. 3:4-5).

3:18—Here James picks up on another of Jesus' beatitudes: "Blessed are the peacemakers, for they will be called sons of God" (Matt. 5:9). They "raise a harvest of righteousness," says James. (For other beatitudes in James, see 1:12, 25.)

GENERAL DISCUSSION

1. Describe someone you would call truly humble.

2. Can you tell how envy and selfish ambition have produced disorder and evil practices in your experience? Explain.

3. How does being considerate relate to being peace-loving? How is being considerate truly an important part of "the humility that comes from wisdom" (James 3:13)?

4. When you view submission as "seeking the welfare of others," how does that clarify your relationships with your employer, your nation, and God? Or doesn't it? If not, why not?

5. Would you agree or disagree that peacemaking is the "core of God's teaching about wisdom"? Why?

6. What is righteousness? How is peacemaking "the seed that produces righteousness"?

SMALL GROUP SESSION IDEAS

Opening (10-15 minutes)

Pray—Open with a prayer for wisdom and understanding as you begin this lesson. You may wish to read Proverbs 4:5-19 or another appropriate Scripture that can help set the tone for this study time.

Share—Share how things are going on the goals or projects you've committed to.

Focus—Throughout this session concentrate on thoughts like these: *How can I show the connection between wisdom and humility more genuinely in my life? How can we do this in the church? In our group?*

Growing (35-40 minutes)

Read (optional)—You may wish to read James 3:13-18 together before moving into your study time. You may also want to read or review portions of the lesson notes.

Discuss—Choose from among the following process questions as you work through questions in the General Discussion section.

- Think of a situation in your day-to-day life in which envy and selfish ambition cause disorder and wrongheaded practices (at work, home, school, church, and so on). In what ways can you help to bring peace and goodness by practicing "the humility that comes from wisdom" (James 3:13)? Share your thoughts with the rest of the group, if you're comfortable doing so.

- Take a few moments to brainstorm together on various ways in which peacemakers have heard God's call to serve and have raised a harvest of righteousness in your community, church, region, or nation.

- Is there someone with whom you need to share James's message about wisdom, humility, peaceloving, and righteousness? Pray about this need, asking for wisdom to know what to say, when to say it, and how to speak God's truth in love.

Goalsetting (5 minutes)

In response to this lesson I want to show God's wisdom more genuinely in my life by committing to . . .

Closing (10-15 minutes)

Preparing for Prayer—Share joys or concerns you'd like to include in the closing prayer.

Prayer—Close with a prayer for wisdom and for the humility that goes with it, showing the true character of wise living for the Lord. Ask the Spirit to help all of us become more and more like Christ, whose example reveals this pattern to all people. Everyone may join in and offer thanks and petitions. Then finish, if you like, by saying together the Lord's Prayer (Matt. 6:9-13).

If you have time, you might also add to your closing a reading of Proverbs 9:1-10, sometimes called "The Invitation of Wisdom."

Group Project (Optional)

Some or all of you may be interested in a cause that works at peacemaking and righteousness in our world today. For ideas and help in getting started on a project through which you can express your hope in Christ, check with health, welfare, political action, denominational, and environmental agencies.

For example, you could help in a local immunization clinic, a blood drive, or a food program. Or you could help clean up a roadway, waterway, or disaster site. Or you could work toward human rights, legal justice, AIDS relief, community safety, literacy and basic-skills education, biblical literacy, acceptance and education of mentally impaired persons, responsible medical research, preservation of wildlife, proper use of land, cleaner air and water—whatever you can think of. Every area of our lives and of this world is under Christ's authority, and he calls us to seek God's kingdom and righteousness even as we live in this world (Deut. 20:19-20; 22:6-7; Ps. 24:1-2; Matt. 6:33; Luke 12:31; Eph. 1:9-10; Rev. 22:1-2).

"Gimme never gets" but sin and trouble.

7

JAMES 4

Warring Against God's Will

In a Nutshell

As we study James 4, we (re)discover that selfishness—unlike true humility (lesson 6)—puts us at war with God's will for us as servants of the kingdom. Our naturally sinful tendencies toward greed and envy must give way to God's grace. One reason this is important is that greed and envy deeply undermine our relationships with others. And the way we relate to others is a key mark of our maturity in faith.

James 4

¹What causes fights and quarrels among you? Don't they come from your desires that battle within you? ²You want something but don't get it. You kill and covet, but you cannot have what you want. You quarrel and fight. You do not have, because you do not ask God. ³When you ask, you do not receive, because you ask with wrong motives, that you may spend what you get on your pleasures.

⁴You adulterous people, don't you know that friendship with the world is hatred toward God? Anyone who chooses to be a friend of the world becomes an enemy of God. ⁵Or do you think Scripture says without reason that the spirit he caused to live in us envies intensely? ⁶But he gives us more grace. That is why Scripture says:

"God opposes the proud
    but gives grace to the humble."

⁷Submit yourselves, then, to God. Resist the devil, and he will flee from you. ⁸Come near to God and he will come near to you. Wash your hands, you sinners, and purify your hearts, you double-minded. ⁹Grieve, mourn and wail. Change your laughter to mourning and your joy to gloom. ¹⁰Humble yourselves before the Lord, and he will lift you up.

¹¹Brothers, do not slander one another. Anyone who speaks against his brother or judges him speaks against the law and judges it. When you judge the law, you are not keeping it, but sitting in judgment on it. ¹²There is only one Lawgiver and Judge, the one who is able to save and destroy. But you—who are you to judge your neighbor?

¹³Now listen, you who say, "Today or tomorrow we will go to this or that city, spend a year there, carry on business and make money." ¹⁴Why, you do not even know what will happen tomorrow. What is your life? You are a mist that appears for a little while and then vanishes. ¹⁵Instead, you ought to say, "If it is the Lord's will, we will live and do this or that." ¹⁶As it is, you boast and brag. All such boasting is evil. ¹⁷Anyone, then, who knows the good he ought to do and doesn't do it, sins.

Quarreling and Fighting

I remember riding the bus to school as a child. It was a small old bus, and there were a lot of children to pick up before we reached our school. By the time we pulled up to the building, not only the rickety seats but also the aisles and doorway were crowded with bodies. (I'm glad the laws about how a bus may be loaded have changed since those days.) As long as everyone sat or stood quietly, everything was fine. But if someone tried to get to the door early, pandemonium broke loose. Elbows pushed here. Knees jerked and feet kicked there. Lots of bruises and nicks soon appeared on small bodies.

In our reading for this lesson, James raises the issue of fights and quarrels among Christians, and he points out that the cause is overcrowding. It's not that there are too many believers in one place but that there are too many misplaced desires within believers' hearts (James 4:1). James sees the source of many quarrels among Christians as greed—greed at war within the individual Christian's life. The idea here is of a life filled with many "I wants" and "I wish I could haves." All these are pushing and shoving each other in the human mind. In 4:2 James gives the example of a person who always wants more. The desire for things is so strong that the person's spirit becomes one of anger, bitterness, and frustration. These emotions lead to quarreling and fighting.

In 4:2 it's unlikely that James is referring to an actual example of murder, but he is forcefully setting out the results of a grabbing mentality for all to see. One result is unceasing envy, jealousy, greed, and fighting within the church. These violent attitudes can destroy believers' sense of worth and the effectiveness of ministry. Murder of the body is not much more evil than destruction of the spirit.

Wrong Focus

James adds that his readers may not have all they want because they have looked to the wrong source and had the wrong motives. The last part of 4:2 implies that these believers have slipped from a secure reliance on God. "You do not have, because you do not ask God," says James. But does this mean they should expect God to make them rich? No. James is emphasizing here that people become more and more greedy as they trust God less and less to give them what they need. They become so focused on what they want that they can only tell God what they want him to do; they lose the wisdom to ask God for what is best (4:3-4). Remember that James's purpose in this letter is to instruct Christians so that even in times of trial God is their heart's desire (1:2-8). Christians must constantly remind each other that life is not about finding pleasure but about God's kingdom and Christ's honor.

The Trouble with Greed and Envy

But really, now, how important is all this business anyway? As long as we trust and honor our Lord, how bad is a little greed and envy? Very bad. Disastrous. James does not beat around the bush on this issue. Believers who allow desire for worldly things to gain a foothold in their lives have committed adultery against the love of God (4:4).

Speaking out within a culture that killed adulterers (see Lev. 20:10), James makes clear that adultery against God's love is no minor matter. To put it frankly, our rejection of God's love is what drove the spikes into Jesus' flesh. Loving the world (that is, courting the forces of self-pleasure and greed) is "hatred toward God" (4:4). Allowing ourselves to be directed to self-pleasure and greed is to align ourselves with the forces working against Christ.

Instead, as James 4:5 indicates, we who have the Spirit of Christ living in us must keep struggling against a sinful spirit within us that continually wants what others have. None of us should think we are above this struggle. Greed and envy are extremely dangerous to our spiritual lives and are universally widespread.

Resisting Temptation

Temptation and sin, however, do not have the last word. The Christian who struggles in humility against the tendency toward greed and friendship with the world has all the resources of God's amazing grace (4:6). Forgiveness and power to change are freely available by the saving work of Christ. And one way to approach the fight is to renew one's resolve to follow God's will (4:7). Instead of fighting and quarreling, Christians should be involved in encouraging one another toward full living in God's kingdom.

Further, the Christian must work to recognize temptations, discerning them not as neutral options but as the work of Satan. Then the Christian must resist. What's more, he or she must understand that resisting temptation is not just a mental resolve. It's a decision and action to change direction and behavior. Doing this takes great strength, so it also takes prayer. As James notes in 4:8, resistance calls for increasing our reliance on God and our communion with God. The only way to resist the devil is to seek the presence of God. We need to center our living on God's Word and prayer. And God will surely visit us with his presence.

The second part of 4:8 begins a summary in the form of a proverb or parable. It calls the Christian to purify outward actions and inward motivations. The believer who has been out of touch with God is to reawaken the truth that, in Christ, one's old life of ungodliness has died. "Grieve, mourn and wail" in repentance anew, says James (4:9).

Of course, as Christians, we don't always have to be serious and mournful because of sin (see 1:2). But we must develop a deep and serious desire for forgiveness. We must truly confess that we still often tend to rely on the things of this world instead of on God, our Savior. When we make this honest confession of our sin in true humility and trust before God, we find the strength of God becoming more and more real in our living as God's people in Christ (4:9-10).

Watching What We Say

James next focuses our attention on what we say about others and to others (4:11-12). Practicing common courtesies and etiquette brings definite benefits in relationships. Small gestures of courtesy can open the way to showing deeper care, concern, and love. But any actions, small or large, that are undermined by evil words are empty at best and can be downright destructive.

For example, we should not slander another person—that is, we should not deliberately spread false information about someone (4:11). And this includes, of course, spreading information that's believed to be true but is not backed by solid evidence.

What's more, we must remember that the "law that gives freedom" (2:12) calls us to love our neighbors. If we do something that brings hurt to others, by our actions we are saying, "It's really not so bad to hurt others." But that shows a marked disagreement with both the Old Testament laws and the New Testament law of love. It shows that we "judge the law" to be in error (4:11). And if we do that, we show that we are going against God's will, or becoming a law unto ourselves. James points out, however, that God is the only one with wisdom and authority to give law and pass judgment, thus giving direction to human life (4:12). God's will, expressed in the heart of the gospel and the law as *love*, is the only direction worth pursuing in life. And speaking falsehood or rumor is hurtful to others, not loving. Those who desire to mature in Christ must discipline themselves in what they say.

Planning Within God's Will

Proceeding with the theme of walking in God's will, James raises the problem of setting a course for our lives without including God (4:13-17). We all need to plan, of course. The saying "If you fail to plan, you plan to fail" has become a hallmark of our times in the work of Christian churches as well as in the business world. But there's a limit to our wisdom that should constantly hold us in check. Despite all our planning, none of us can forecast what will happen even one day into the future (4:14). And whether we like it or not, we are inherently weak and vulnerable in the way we are made. Every one of us is alive only briefly. We do not have the wisdom to make a final plan for our best welfare. And we do not have the power to ensure that even the plans we can make will be carried out.

The alternative is to shape our decisions around a conscious awareness of the true God (4:15). Having seen God's loving will for our lives in the resurrection of Christ our Lord, we can rest in that will. As we plan our living, we should constantly be shaping our plans according to God's loving will and desiring God's will to overrule our plans.

To ignore God or to relegate God to a corner of life away from our daily planning is to "boast and brag" (4:16). If we slip into such self-sufficient behavior, we put God in a position of waiting on the sidelines while we pursue our own selfish ends. That kind of behavior is not neutral at all. It is anti-God, un-Christian, "evil" (4:16). Instead of boasting and bragging, we must keep our ears open to God's Word and to God's people around us. Listening, practiced with prayer, will enable us to grow in planning within God's will.

But we still must expect God to bring us the surprises of grace. We must always look for God's love and direction in the unfolding course of our living. James 4:17 summarizes by saying we must do what we know to be right. If we expect God to lead our living and yet do not act accordingly, we are living in sin.

Additional Notes

4:1—The Greek word for "desires" (*hedone*) also gives us the term *hedonism*, which means "the pursuit of pleasure." Another form of the word occurs again in 4:3, where it is translated as "pleasures."

4:2—From the context here we can see that "you kill" does not refer to physical murder but that we should view it as another way of saying "you hate." Jesus himself teaches that hating someone is like murdering that person in your heart (Matt. 5:21-22; see also 1 John 3:15). Further, the verb joined with "you kill" in James 4:2 is "covet," a word that clearly designates a sin of the heart.

4:3—The word for "ask" here (*aiteo*) is the same one Jesus uses when he says, "Ask and it will be given you" (Matt. 7:7). In a way similar to Jesus' teaching in another passage that uses the same word for "ask" (John 15:7), James 4 explains that we will receive what we ask for when we ask for all we truly need in line with God's will.

4:4—Note John's similar statement in 1 John 2:15: "If anyone loves the world, the love of the Father is not in him." Both John and James establish that we must love either God or the world. We cannot love both. (See also Matt. 6:19-24.)

4:5—James claims that according to the Old Testament, the spirit that God placed in us has a natural tendency toward envy (but note also the alternate translations in a footnote in the NIV). Assuming that the NIV text has the correct interpretation, where in the Old Testament do we read about this natural tendency? Perhaps James had in mind Genesis 4:7, where God tells Cain that if he does not guard against his feelings of envy toward Abel, sin will get the better of him. Or perhaps James was thinking of Genesis 6:5, which says God looked on human wickedness and saw that "every inclination of the thoughts of [humanity's] heart was only evil all the time."

4:7—The prime example of resisting the devil is the Lord Jesus. In full submission to his Father's will as revealed in Scripture, Jesus did not yield to Satan's temptations in the desert, so "the devil left him" (Matt. 4:11). James implies that his readers' spiritual unfaithfulness (4:4) is the result of yielding to the devil's influence.

4:8—What a powerful promise: if we draw near to God (see Isa. 55:6-7), God will fill our lives with his presence. The Greek word for "double-minded" (*dipsychos*) is the same as the one used in 1:8, but here it refers not to someone who is doubting but to someone who is trying to love both God and the pleasures of the world.

4:10—James here picks up a teaching from Proverbs 3:34 (see also James 4:6) to reinforce a principle that Jesus spoke on several occasions: those who humble themselves before the

Lord will be exalted (see Matt. 23:12; Luke 14:11; 18:14). This same theme is echoed in the Song of Mary in Luke 1:52.

GENERAL DISCUSSION

1. Not just clothes, cars, and money can become the focus of our greed. Pick a partner and list a few ways in which you think greed for power, information, and control can affect the church. Then list other evidences of greed in our lifestyles today. Share your answers with the rest of the group.

2. Why do we so love money and what it can buy? Do you think things themselves have a power toward evil, as "the love of money" does (see 1 Tim. 6:10)? Why?

3. List ten things you can do to work against envy and greed in your life.

4. What guidelines do you think Christians should follow to determine whether something should be said or repeated about another person?

5. How can Christians shape their plans according to God's will?

SMALL GROUP SESSION IDEAS

Opening (10-15 minutes)

Pray—Ask the Holy Spirit to help each of you see more clearly during this session what it means to live by God's will. Consider also saying the Lord's Prayer together (Matt. 6:9-13), reflecting thoughtfully on the meaning of each petition in this model prayer that Jesus taught his disciples.

Share—Share how things are going on goals or projects you've committed to.

Focus—Keep in mind the following focus question throughout this session: *In what ways might I be going against God's will in my daily living?*

Growing (35-40 minutes)

Read (optional)—You may find it helpful to read James 4 together before discussing the lesson material. You may also want to read or review portions of the lesson notes.

Discuss—Choose from among the following questions as you work through the General Discussion section.

- What effects do "fights and quarrels" in the church have on you? How about in your family? In your workplace or neighborhood? In what ways do these disturbances affect your ability to serve God?

- Are you someone who lives every day with the thought that it may be your last? If not, how would your life and relationships be different if you lived that way?

- Have you ever made plans that you knew were against God's will? What happened? Share your experience with the rest of the group, if you are comfortable doing so.

Goalsetting (5 minutes)

As a result of this lesson I want to try to live more faithfully in line with God's will. Here's what I want to do:

Closing (10-15 minutes)

Preparing for Prayer—Mention joys or concerns you'd like to share before you close in prayer together.

Prayer—Ask the Holy Spirit to fill each one of you anew with a desire to live faithfully within God's will, and to grant you the strength each day to do so. Everyone may join in with personal petitions or praises. Ask also for God's guidance in sharing with others what it means to come near to God and resist the temptations of the devil.

If your group likes singing, you might also wish to sing "Spirit of the Living God" before parting.

When Jesus
comes, will he
find us
faithful?

8

JAMES 5:1-12

Trusting the Truth of God

In a Nutshell

God does not intend for Christ's churches to stand still. James indicates that in all things God is working to move churches as well as individual believers to a greater maturity in living the Christlike life. So it's important to pursue God's will (rather than riches), to practice patience, and to persevere in trusting God's truth. In God's strength we can do these things, proclaiming new life in Christ until he comes.

James 5:1-12

¹Now listen, you rich people, weep and wail because of the misery that is coming upon you. ²Your wealth has rotted, and moths have eaten your clothes. ³Your gold and silver are corroded. Their corrosion will testify against you and eat your flesh like fire. You have hoarded wealth in the last days. ⁴Look! The wages you failed to pay the workmen who mowed your fields are crying out against you. The cries of the harvesters have reached the ears of the Lord Almighty. ⁵You have lived on earth in luxury and self-indulgence. You have fattened yourselves in the day of slaughter. ⁶You have condemned and murdered innocent men, who were not opposing you.

⁷Be patient, then, brothers, until the Lord's coming. See how the farmer waits for the land to yield its valuable crop and how patient he is for the autumn and spring rains. ⁸You too, be patient and stand firm, because the Lord's coming is near. ⁹Don't grumble against each other, brothers, or you will be judged. The Judge is standing at the door!

¹⁰Brothers, as an example of patience in the face of suffering, take the prophets who spoke in the name of the Lord. ¹¹As you know, we consider blessed those who have persevered. You have heard of Job's perseverance and have seen what the Lord finally brought about. The Lord is full of compassion and mercy.

¹²Above all, my brothers, do not swear —not by heaven or by earth or by anything else. Let your "Yes" be yes, and your "No," no, or you will be condemned.

Avoiding the Pitfalls of Living for Wealth

Learning God's will, shaping our living according to that will, and trusting God's grace—all lead James to write next about a particular problem among his first readers. It seems that a number of James's readers were wealthy Christians, and it was clear that these people had gained their wealth in less-than-godly ways.

James declares that these people will one day be in misery, and because of that coming misery, they should also be miserable now (5:1). One reason for their misery is that all the things they have placed their trust in are temporary (5:2-3). The things that money can buy are a poor crutch to lean on as we walk into the days ahead. Things lose their value—more quickly than we imagine.

A second reason why these rich people should be miserable, says James, is that they are often destroyed as their wealth loses its power (5:3). Yet another reason is that these rich have amassed and kept wealth "in the last days" (5:3). This phrase is a common New Testament term referring to the time after Jesus' resurrection, and it points to the expectation that Jesus will soon return. Jesus' finished work has turned history toward its end. In the New Testament way of thinking, the resurrection has changed the very meaning and direction of life. In this time of renewed value and purpose, James is rebuking rich Christians who have focused on saving money. In days that should be marked by the serving life of Christ, these rich have chosen to keep and spend rather than to give and serve.

Wealth is too often gained at the expense of others (5:4). Not only does hoarding wealth work against God's will in the resurrection life of Christian believers, but gaining wealth unfairly also causes great harm. We must always pay workers what we have promised so that others will not suffer because of us. We must know that God hears those who are hurt and will avenge them.

James closes this section with a summary in the form of three accusations (5:5-6). Every Christian is wise to listen carefully to these statements and to search his or her own heart. First, some people live a life focused on getting what they want for themselves. As a result, they establish, as much as possible, a life without hardships. They avoid trials at any cost. (Note how this pursuit conflicts with James's main point that growth in faith comes through trial.) Second, these people have gained while the world around them has fallen apart. In the face of great need they have settled for gathering treasure. Third, they have been an active part in the harm that has come to others, even though there has been no opposition from those others.

Those who want to walk in the power of the resurrection must actively trust in and pursue the will of God.

Practicing Patience

At this point James strongly encourages patience as a necessary Christian virtue. He says it's like the patience farmers need as they wait for seasonal rains (5:7). I've been told that in the Middle East farmers need an autumn rain to soften the soil for planting and a spring rain to fill out the crops for harvest. No good crops are possible during the fierce summer heat and dryness there. James was obviously familiar with this cycle of need and waiting.

Christians are to be patient in practice, especially because they live in the reality that the Lord is coming soon (5:8). One aspect of this teaching is that people might give up on the faith, having lost patience during trial. *Patience* has been defined as "calmly tolerating delay." James is encouraging Christians here to tolerate delay rather than give up hope. When relief is delayed, we must hold more securely to the truth of God that holds securely to us.

Another aspect of this teaching is that Christians might act impatiently toward each other, especially in perceiving how others are maturing as God's imagebearers. James is encouraging Christians to remember that we want to be doing right in these days when the resurrected Jesus will soon return. Acting harshly does not move ahead the mission of Jesus' return. Christians must not try to rush God's timing or purposes but must hold securely to God's truth.

In light of all this, the Christian must not develop a negative attitude or speak negatively about other Christians (5:9). Grumbling is a major divider and a force against progress in the church. God does not intend for Christ's churches to stand still. James indicates clearly that in all things God is working to move churches as well as individuals to a greater and greater maturity in trust and in living the Christlike life. But if we become intolerant and grumbly because our plans or expectations are not fulfilled, the progress of the church is greatly hampered.

It's important to remember that we cannot grumble and be negative without also judging (5:9). When we grumble, we hold up a measuring device, saying, "Well, you haven't met the mark." But as James points out in earlier parts of his letter, if we operate in the context of judgment, we can expect judgment ourselves. If we insist on judgment rather than hope, trust, and grace, we will be judged as relentless taskmasters.

The close of 5:9 emphasizes the choice of perspective that can shape our lives. Jesus' second coming will in fact happen at any moment. He will come and judge between right and wrong, truth and error. But we can see him not only as the Judge but also as the source of life, forgiveness, hope, and joy. If we can see Christ that way, we can be patient when our plans go awry and when others do not do as we've expected. We can trust the truth of God and greet trials with joy rather than with impatience and grumbling.

Persevering in Trust

To reinforce the importance of patience in Christian living, especially in times of suffering, James adds that the prophets of the Old Testament showed great patience through trial in their lives (5:10). Moses' authority was questioned and opposed. Elijah often had to flee for his life. Jeremiah was imprisoned for resolutely declaring God's message. Hosea was ordered to marry a prostitute. Yet all these prophets continued to live and speak in trust of God's purposes and Word.

The key to being blessed is to see that any trial is worth the reward of growth in the Lord. To persevere in trust in the face of events that work against our plans and comfort is the heart of true happiness (5:11; see Matt. 5:11-12). Holding on, by action and word, to the truth of one's hope in Christ is the source of joy in the face of temptation and opposition.

James lifts up the situation of Job as an example for our lives. Theologian J. A. Motyer points out that the focus of this example is not so much Job's steadfastness as God's purposefulness. The phrase "what the Lord finally brought about" (5:11) could also be translated as "the Lord's purposes." Motyer states that the end of Job "was . . . the chosen divine objective from the beginning. Above all else it was the enrichment of knowing God more fully. Job ended with a greater testimony than he had ever had before." In Job 42:5 we find Job saying, "My ears had heard of you but now my eyes have seen you." Motyer adds that James emphasizes "what came to be freshly known about God, how the Lord is compassionate and merciful." This is exactly what the Christian community had learned through the death and resurrection of Christ. And this is exactly the truth that grows through trial in the life of faith. "The Lord is full of compassion and mercy" (James 5:11). This truth not only makes patience possible but also demands patience in the life of every believer.

Trusting in God's Truth

At first it may seem that James's mind has wandered at 5:12 or that perhaps someone else has tucked a little advice into this letter. But when we look closer, it becomes clear that James is saying that swearing, or taking oaths, shows we are really trusting in our own way, our own ideas, our own "truth." James may have been addressing an actual instance of swearing that showed a lack of patient perseverance. James's point is that in taking an oath, we are not resting in the truth that can defend itself. We may feel we need to back up our "truth" with swearing because we sense that the "truth" we are speaking cannot stand on its own. The problem, though, is that we have a habit of not resting in and speaking the truth of God. So our swearing is an attempt to say, "No, I have not been trustworthy, but, even so, I really want my way!"

James calls for an approach that is trusting and is therefore trustworthy. The Christian who grows in faith in the Lord will be known for patient trust in truth. Our speech patterns are a critical sign of our trust and of the way of life we are walking in. The woman or man of faith must be a person of straightforward truth. To be less is to trust less, to hope less, and to witness to less. The Lord who gives our lives their meaning will indeed deal with those who settle for less (5:12).

Additional Notes

5:2-3—James's words appear to be adapted from Jesus' Sermon on the Mount (see Matt. 6:19-21). The rich have stored up so much wealth that it has rotted or been eaten by moths, meaning that it has been in disuse. So we should ask ourselves, "Is it right to have our attics full of stuff subject to moths and decay, when it could be used profitably by someone who has little or nothing?" Anytime we allow something to get corroded through disuse, it testifies against us, says James (5:3).

5:6—The Greek word for "innocent" is most often translated in other passages as "righteous" (see also the NRSV translation of 5:6). It appears that the people whom the rich were treating shamefully were believers—that is, those who were righteous in Christ.

5:8—The Greek phrase for "stand firm" literally means "strengthen your hearts." In other words, be determined; have a strong inner resolve. Patience and perseverance require a strong inner resolve. It's easy to lose our sense of composure in times of trouble.

5:10—Probably no prophet had more reason to grumble than Jeremiah did. Yet he persevered in his ministry to the unfaithful Israelites around him.

5:11—The Greek phrase for "we consider blessed" uses the same wording we find in the beatitudes: "Blessed are . . ." (Matt. 5:3-12). This phrase in James 5:11 relates back to the beatitude in 1:12: "Blessed is the man who perseveres under trial." The words for "persevered" and "perseverance" in 5:11 (in reference to Job; sometimes translated as "patience") come from a word group that literally means "to rest or remain under." Job *remained* firm in his commitment to the Lord *under* the most trying of circumstances. We ought to do the same.

GENERAL DISCUSSION

1. Can a person be rich and still live as a Christian? Explain.

2. What are some ways in which we withhold payment and hoard goods? Who might be suffering because we do this?

3. In what ways do we need to be patient in our growth toward maturity as God's imagebearers? (See James 5:7-9.) What is the truth that makes patience possible?

4. What really makes you lose your patience? What would it mean in this situation to trust God more?

5. Why do you think James often warns us against the consequences of judging others? (See James 2:4, 13; 3:1; 4:11; 5:9.)

6. What events in your life show God's compassion, mercy, and desire that you know God? What attitudes and actions do these events seem to demand from you if you persevere in trust?

7. Outside of the courtroom, where are people most likely to use an oath? What would such an oath say about a person's trust?

SMALL GROUP SESSION IDEAS

Opening (10-15 minutes)
Pray—As you begin this session, pray for the strength to trust in God and be faithful, no matter what trials or challenges may come. Ask for the grace to keep God's "big picture" in mind and to look daily for the Lord's return. At this time you may also wish to reflect together on a reading of Psalm 40:1-8.

Share—Share how things are going on goals or projects you've committed to.

Focus—During this session try to focus on the following thoughts: *Am I involved in any wrongdoing through a misuse of wealth, mistreatment of others, or mistrust in God? If so, what can I do to change that behavior?*

Growing (35-40 minutes)
Read (optional)—You may wish to read James 5:1-12 together as you move into your discussion time. You may also want to read or review portions of the lesson notes.

Discuss—Use some or all of these process questions as you wish while working through the General Discussion questions.

- Think of someone you know or know of who is wealthy and is also a devoted Christian. In what ways does this person use the gifts of wealth and power to serve God in this world? In what ways can you or do you use your own wealth and power to serve God?

- Think of someone you know or know of who has shown a good example of godly patience in the face of suffering or trial. Perhaps this is a person who's been persecuted for his or her faith in Christ. Or maybe it's someone with a terminal illness who has drawn deeply from God's strength and has shown remarkable perseverance and trust in God. Describe the effect this person's example has had on you.

• Think of at least a few ways in which you can show others, by both your speech and actions, how to live in the hope of the Lord's coming and in the light of God's coming kingdom.

Goalsetting (5 minutes)

I want to work at being more in tune with God's "big picture" as I live here on this earth. Here's what I'd like to do:

Closing (10-15 minutes)

Preparing for Prayer—Mention joys or concerns you'd like to bring before the Lord as you close in prayer together.

Prayer—Ask for guidance as you seek each day to live in the light of God's coming kingdom, and for strength to be patient and to persevere, especially in the face of hardships and suffering. Everyone may join in with personal joys or concerns. Then end your prayer by reading together the following lines from *Our World Belongs to God: A Contemporary Testimony* (st. 57-58):

> We long for that day
> when Jesus will return as triumphant King,
> when the dead will be raised
> and all people will stand before his judgment.
> We face that day without fear,
> for the Judge is our Savior.
> Our daily lives of service aim for the moment
> when the Son will present his people to the Father.
> Then God will be shown to be true, holy, and
> gracious. . . .
>
> With the whole creation
> we wait for the purifying fire of judgment.
> For then we will see the Lord face to face.
> He will heal our hurts,
> end our wars,

and make the crooked straight. . . .
God will be all in all,
righteousness and peace will flourish,
everything will be made new,
and every eye will see at last
that our world belongs to God!
Hallelujah! Come, Lord Jesus.

Group Project (Optional)

For some ideas that can help you get into living and working in the hope of God's coming kingdom, see the group project suggestions at the end of session 6.

*Trusting in
God through
Jesus brings
real life.*

9

JAMES 5:13-20

Prayer and Mercy

In a Nutshell

James wants the maturing faith of Christ's people to be evident in deed as well as in feeling and attitude—in all settings. So now James addresses a variety of situations, suggesting ways in which believers can give evidence of their growing faith, showing that the life of God in them is real.

James 5:13-20

13Is any one of you in trouble? He should pray. Is anyone happy? Let him sing songs of praise. 14Is any one of you sick? He should call the elders of the church to pray over him and anoint him with oil in the name of the Lord. 15And the prayer offered in faith will make the sick person well; the Lord will raise him up. If he has sinned, he will be forgiven. 16Therefore confess your sins to each other and pray for each other so that you may be healed. The prayer of a righteous man is powerful and effective.

17Elijah was a man just like us. He prayed earnestly that it would not rain, and it did not rain on the land for three and a half years. 18Again he prayed, and the heavens gave rain, and the earth produced its crops.

19My brothers, if one of you should wander from the truth and someone should bring him back, 20remember this: Whoever turns a sinner from the error of his way will save him from death and cover over a multitude of sins.

Not Getting Sidetracked

Sometimes my thoughts run ahead of my mouth. My children have been known to complain, "What is he talking about?" while I'm answering a perfectly simple question. Well, let me just say that it's not that I can't stick to the point, but sometimes my mind makes a lot of side trips in getting to the point.

It may seem that James too gets sidetracked as his letter draws to a close. Suddenly in 5:13 he starts talking about prayer, singing, elders, confession, and forgiveness. But James has not wandered mentally.

Pray, Praise, Trust

From the start of his letter James's concern has been that Christians' trust in their Lord will come alive and grow—in all circumstances. James wants the maturing faith of Christ's people to be evident in deed as well as in feeling and attitude—in all settings. So now James addresses the possibility that there might be real trouble in the lives of the Christians he is writing to. Or maybe there's a cause for celebration. Or perhaps someone or several persons at once are seriously ill. In each situation James suggests a way that the believer can give evidence of a growing faith. In whatever your circumstances, he seems to say, find a way to deepen your trust in God. Earnestly desire to draw closer to your Lord.

If there's trouble anywhere (James 5:13), direct yourselves consciously toward God. Become more and more aware of the love and mercy of God in Christ. Pray.

Have you received some blessing to be happy about? Show your maturing joy in ways that not only show beauty and creativity but also clearly proclaim the source of your joy. Sing praise to God.

Is there sickness in your community? Once again the main point here must be seen as a call to reliance on God. James 5:14-15 is not a "cookbook for healing," as if James is suddenly putting forward a new formula (or law) for gaining God's favor. The direction is the same as in 5:13—and indeed as in the entire letter: in all your circumstances turn consciously to God, who guides your life's destiny. In times of need, one should consciously turn toward the people of God—and especially their leaders (elders).

Just what "anoint . . . with oil" means in 5:14 has often been hotly debated. It may refer to a form of accepted medical treatment in James's day (see Mark 6:13; Luke 10:34). It may refer to a ceremony of dedication symbolizing trust in God (see Ex. 30:22-33; Ps. 133:2). Some say it's a religiously significant step in the healing process. Most important, though, is to bear in mind that the crucial direction is found in the words "in the name of the Lord" (James 5:14). What's critical here is trust in the Lord and growth in the community of faith. Only in the name of the living Lord can one pass through trials with joy. And only God's love can turn a trial into an event of growth in maturing trust and obedience.

James is unafraid to challenge growing Christians to expect miracles. When we pray in faith, we can look for healing, for the growth in wholeness that we seek (5:15). Because of God's mercy, we can look for an end to our pain and suffering. But, even more, we can expect to grow closer to God through our suffering.

Pray for and Confess to Each Other

In 5:16 James calls us to pray for each other's forgiveness. It's important that each of us seeks to deepen our trust and fellowship in God, so we also must desire this for each other. We must pray for each other, seeking above all the deeper fellowship with God that comes through forgiveness. In line with this mutual prayer James also calls us to mutual confession. This injunction stands directly against the mutual criticism (slander, grumbling, and complaining) that at least some of James's readers have been guilty of (4:11-12; 5:9). James's call for deeper, more mature, more alive faith runs throughout this letter, and it speaks out strongly here.

Pray Fervently Within God's Will

James also urges us to greater faith and expectation in our dialogue with God. When we read about the prayer of a righteous person (5:16), we must remember that all in Christ are righteous (Rom. 4:18-25). James is not saying there are some special standards of goodness necessary for prayer to be heard. Each and every person who trusts in Jesus as Savior and Lord is considered righteous and is accepted into the presence of God. It is the prayer of every true believer, then, that is "powerful and effective." Prayer is powerful in that it helps to keep us connected with God, whose power can accomplish great things. Through prayer and by God's powerful mercy, situations change. Healing becomes real. Hope appears and grows. Forgiveness spreads. Prayer is effective in that it gets to the point. What is truly needed is provided. What is truly desired in line with God's will in Christ becomes actual. Prayer brings people closer to the way of our Lord.

Elijah is a good example of a person "just like us" (James 5:17). He had trials and real doubts. He had needs and fears. But through it all he trusted in God's word and promise. Elijah was ordinary, but he was God's child. His prayer was the powerful, effective, yet ordinary prayer of a person of faith. When he prayed, the rain stopped. And when he prayed again, the rain came. It's important to note here that the prayers for and against rain were God's idea. God wanted the rain stopped, and God promised that the rain would come (see 1 Kings 17:1-7; 18:1-2, 41-46). So James is giving us a picture of a person of faith praying earnestly for what he knew was within God's purpose and desire. It's also important to note how fervently Elijah prayed for rain to come, even when he knew God had promised it. Elijah's was a fervent, repeated prayer for something that was clearly God's desire. Most important, though, is that Elijah's example points out the certainty of God's answer to the ordinary prayer of faith. When the righteous in Christ call, will he not answer? (See Ps. 40:1; 145:17-19; Rom. 10:12-13.)

Live the Real Life

The issue of life is faith. Trusting in God through Jesus brings real life. Living in Christ as we pass through the trials and challenges of this world matures and deepens our faith. What greater love could we offer to any brother or sister than to bring him or her back to this truth (James 5:19)? In this letter James has called to people who may be wandering from a living trust in God because of sufferings and hard times they've had to face. James has urged a renewed trust that is shown and supported by a vibrant life of faith and humility.

And now he turns the task over to us. Strengthening the trust of a wavering sister or brother will cover many wrongs (5:20). It will enable the person to find new life, purpose, and hope. It will enable us to grow in understanding, love, and humility. This is what life in Christ is all about, that in all events and situations we may grow in the life that overwhelms us with deep joy as we grow deeper and deeper in our trust in the Lord.

Additional Notes

5:13—The Greek word for "in trouble" (*kakopatheo*) is from the same root as the word describing the "suffering" of the prophets in 5:10.

5:14—Of the two activities that elders might perform for a sick person, the more critical one is praying. In the Greek text, the idea of anointing with oil is introduced in a subordinate participial construction, while the idea of praying is the main verb in this part of the sentence. Regardless of whether the oil is medicinal or symbolizes something spiritual, it will be effective only if given in the name of the Lord.

5:15—Even though the Greek verb for "will raise" (*egerei*) is similar to the word that describes the raising of Jesus from the dead (Mark 16:6; Luke 24:6), the meaning here is that the sick person will be able to get up from his or her sick bed. Further, this person's sins will be forgiven. More and more today doctors are rediscovering the role that a person's spiritual health plays in his or her physical well-being. In many cases, a person recovers much more quickly if his or her relationship is right with the Lord.

5:17-18—Two features stand out in James's description of Elijah. (1) He was an ordinary person just like each one of us. He had his failures, shortcomings, and weaknesses (note his depression and desire to die—1 Kings 19:3-6). So, as James implies, we should not deify Elijah to the extent that we do not dare pray as he did. He was, just as we are, a mere human being. (2) He was righteous (implied from James 5:16). This does not mean Elijah was better than we are; rather, his righteousness means that he was considered righteous by God because he was thoroughly committed to God Almighty (see Gen. 15:6). And that's the same way we can be considered righteous, for when we believe in the Lord Jesus Christ, we are justified (that is, we become righteous—Rom. 3:21-26).

The key element to the "success" of Elijah's prayers was his desire to glorify God (recall James's comments on "unsuccessful" prayer in 4:2-3). Elijah wanted God's name and God's kingdom to flourish (note especially 1 Kings 17:17-24; 18:36-39). Even Elijah's prayer to die was not for personal, selfish blessing; it stemmed from his frustration at not being able to uproot the worship of Baal from Israel for the Lord's sake. Our basis for prayer should be the same as Elijah's—to desire intensely that God and his kingdom will reign supreme.

5:19-20—Once again James addresses his readers as "brothers," as fellow believers in Christ. James is concerned here about believers who "wander from the truth," like the wandering sheep in Jesus' parable in Matthew 18:10-14 (see also Luke 15:4-7). We all have a responsibility to watch out for one another and to nudge each other to walk carefully in the Christian way of life. Discipline in the church is not just the responsibility of official church leaders; unless the entire church is a part of the process, it will usually fail (see 1 Cor. 5:1-5). The point to emphasize in any disciplinary situation is that the Lord's love and forgiveness are bountiful (see Ps. 103:8-12). As the wise teacher says in Proverbs 10:12, "Love [especially the love of the Lord] covers over all wrongs."

GENERAL DISCUSSION

1. Do you think praise to God is better expressed in simple terms or in some explanation of the meaning and source of our hope? Explain. (See James 5:13.)

2. In what ways does God give healing in response to our prayers for the sick? When might God not give this answer to our prayers? (See Ps. 66:18; Heb. 12:5-8; James 1:2-7; 4:3.)

3. In what manner and setting do you think Christians should confess their sins to one another? To what extent do you think they should "bare their souls"?

4. What are some things that you know God desires? When have you heard or said prayers for these things? How do we know when our prayers are fervent enough?

5. Now that you've reached the end of this study, what would you say truly makes for a living faith?

SMALL GROUP SESSION IDEAS

Opening (10-15 minutes)

Pray—Pray for understanding and a strengthening of faith as you focus during this session on a variety of ways in which we can show that our faith is real. Include petitions for people who are in trouble or in need of healing or are wandering from God. Ask also for an openness to learn new things that the Spirit may want to teach through the Scriptures during this session.

Share—Share how things are going on goals or projects you've committed to.

Focus—Concentrate on one or more of the following questions as you work through this session: *Is there something the Holy Spirit wants to teach me in this passage from James about prayer? About healing? About trusting in God? About showing that my faith is real?*

Growing (35-40 minutes)

Read (optional)—You may wish to read the Scripture for the lesson as you move into your discussion time. You may also want to read or review portions of the lesson notes.

Discuss—Include the following process questions as you work through the General Discussion questions together.

- Think of someone you know or know of for whom the Christian community has prayed for healing. Describe the situation and give examples of the various kinds of healing (physical, emotional, spiritual, relational, and so on) that took place. In what ways did God answer the people's prayers? (For example, did God say, "Yes," "No," "Wait a while longer," "I'll respond in a different way than you expect," or "Not till you confess your sin"?)

- In what ways has God shown you through this study of James how to live more faithfully? How to persevere in times of testing and challenge? How to be more like Jesus? Try to shape your answer in a way that an unchurched person or unbeliever could understand.

- Think of someone who has wandered from the faith. Pray for spiritual healing and new growth in that person's life, and ask God for insights on how to show Jesus' love to that person and to invite him or her back to faithful living. If this is a person whom others in the group also know or know of, you may wish to share your concern and ask them for prayers and insights as well.

Goalsetting (5 minutes)

In response to this study of the book of James, I want to strive to keep growing spiritually and showing that my faith is real. With God's help I want to do this in the following ways:

Closing (10-15 minutes)

Preparing for Prayer—Mention joys or concerns that you'd like to bring before the Lord as you close in prayer together.

Prayer—Thank God for bringing you through this season of Bible study together. Everyone may join in with concerns and praises related to this study and to personal daily living. Ask for God's blessings of strength and faith and perseverance to take what you've learned from James and to show others by your words and actions that your faith in Jesus is real.

Group Study Project (Optional)

If any of you would like to learn more about prayer, you may wish to study it sometime as a group or as individuals. Here's a brief list of resources we recommend on prayer:

- *Teaching P.R.A.Y.E.R.: Guidance for Pastors and Church Leaders* (Abingdon, 2001) by Brant D. Baker

- *Too Busy Not to Pray*, second ed. (InterVarsity, 1998), by Bill Hybels

- *The Praying Church Sourcebook*, second ed. (CRC Publications, 1997), by Alvin J. Vander Griend with Edith Bajema

- *The Praying Church Ideabook: Practical Ways Your Church Can Pray* (Faith Alive Resources, 2001), by Douglas A. Kamstra

- *Developing a Prayer-Care-Share Lifestyle* (HOPE Ministries, 1999), devotions written by Alvin J. Vander Griend, Edith Bajema, John F. DeVries, and David J. Deters

You can learn more about these and other titles at *www.Faith AliveResources.org*, or call 1-800-333-8300 for assistance or for a free catalog.

EVALUATIONS

Please fill out the evaluation form at the back of this study guide. Your answers and suggestions help us as we develop other studies in the *Word Alive* series. Thank you!

Please mail evaluations to

Word Alive/James
Faith Alive Christian Resources
2850 Kalamazoo Ave. SE
Grand Rapids, MI 49560

Bibliography

Alexander, David and Alexander, Patricia, eds. *Eerdmans' Handbook to the Bible*. Grand Rapids, Mich.: Wm. B. Eerdmans, 1973.

Furnish, Victor P. *The Love Command in the New Testament*. New York: Abingdon, 1972.

Harrison, Everett F. *Introduction to the New Testament*. Grand Rapids, Mich.: Wm. B. Eerdmans, 1964.

Kittel, G. *Theological Dictionary of the New Testament*. Grand Rapids, Mich.: Wm. B. Eerdmans, 1965.

Motyer, J. A. *The Test of Faith*. Downers Grove, Ill.: InterVarsity Press, 1970.

Reicke, Bo. *The Anchor Bible*: The Epistles of James, Peter and Jude. Vol. 37. Garden City, N.Y.: Doubleday, 1964.

Tasker, R. V. G., ed. *James*. Tyndale New Testament Commentaries. Grand Rapids, Mich.: Wm. B. Eerdmans, 1976.

Wilson, Earl D. *The Undivided Self*. Downers Grove, Ill.: InterVarsity Press, 1983.

Evaluation

Background
Size of group:
- [ ] fewer than 5 persons
- [ ] 5-10
- [ ] 10-15
- [ ] more than 15

Age of participants:
- [ ] 20-30
- [ ] 31-45
- [ ] 46-60
- [ ] 61-75 or above

Length of group sessions:
- [ ] under 60 minutes
- [ ] 60-75 minutes
- [ ] 75-90 minutes
- [ ] 90-120 minutes or more

Please check items that describe you:
- [ ] male
- [ ] female
- [ ] ordained or professional church staff person
- [ ] elder or deacon
- [ ] professional teacher
- [ ] church school or catechism teacher (three or more years' experience)
- [ ] trained small group leader

Study Guide and Group Process
Please check items that describe the material in the study guide:
- [ ] varied
- [ ] monotonous
- [ ] creative
- [ ] dull
- [ ] clear
- [ ] unclear
- [ ] interesting to participants
- [ ] uninteresting to participants
- [ ] too much
- [ ] too little
- [ ] helpful, stimulating
- [ ] not helpful or stimulating
- [ ] overly complex, long
- [ ] appropriate level of difficulty

Please check items that describe the group sessions:
- [ ] lively
- [ ] dull
- [ ] dominated by leader
- [ ] involved most participants
- [ ] relevant to lives of participants
- [ ] irrelevant to lives of participants
- [ ] worthwhile
- [ ] not worthwhile

In general I would rate this material as

☐ excellent

☐ very good

☐ good

☐ fair

☐ poor

Additional comments on any aspect of this Bible study:

Name (optional): _____

Church: _____

_____

City/State/Province: _____

_____

Please send completed form to

Word Alive/James

Faith Alive Christian Resources

2850 Kalamazoo Ave. SE

Grand Rapids, MI 49560

Thank you!

19

Apr. 2 7:30
Lesson 4 @ My house

Feb. 11   7:30
Lesson 6 @ Hidda's

April 15
7:30 @ Harveys?
Lesson 8